ABANDONED VIRGINIA

FORGOTTEN IN TIME

DAVE BENTLEY

AMERICA THROUGH TIME®
ADDING COLOR TO AMERICAN HISTORY

America Through Time is an imprint of Fonthill Media LLC
www.through-time.com
office@through-time.com

Published by Arcadia Publishing by arrangement with Fonthill Media LLC
For all general information, please contact Arcadia Publishing:
Telephone: 843-853-2070
Fax: 843-853-0044
E-mail: sales@arcadiapublishing.com
For customer service and orders:
Toll-Free 1-888-313-2665

www.arcadiapublishing.com

First published 2021

ISBN 978-1-63499-364-7

Typeset in Trade Gothic 10pt on 15pt
Printed and bound in England

CONTENTS

ACKNOWLEDGMENTS

Over the years, I've had the opportunity to explore hundreds of abandoned locations across the country, and even internationally. While some aren't as picturesque as the rest, I always made it a challenge to find something interesting to document. While photographing and documenting the history of these lost and forgotten places is my main interest, a close second has been the adventure, discovery, and memories made along the way.

Urban exploration can be dangerous, and one of the first rules is to not go alone. I've had the privilege of having some great exploring partners who are excellent photographers in their own right, to whom I owe a lot of credit. This list includes Eric Brown, Lewis Francis, Rob Cox, Brett, and many others. Most of all, my utmost heartfelt appreciation and thanks to my girlfriend and travel/exploring partner, Allison White, who has always supported me, continually encourages me, and pushes me to improve. I couldn't do it without her. And last but not least, to my brother, Johnnie Bentley, sister, Debbie Bentley, and all my friends who have supported me along the way. Thank you.

INTRODUCTION

Urban Exploration can be defined as "the exploration of manmade structures, usually abandoned ruins or hidden components of the manmade environment. Photography and historical interest/documentation are heavily featured in the hobby."

Long before I knew this hobby had a name, I was always interested in the history of those old buildings and the character they possessed. My passion for photographing abandoned places comes from wanting to preserve the history before they're demolished and forgotten forever.

I'd love to see historical buildings repurposed and given a second life, but many times that is unfortunately not the case. Various factors contribute to this, including vandalism and scrapping. This is why you'll find that many explorers will not disclose location details, hoping to protect these sites. These are guidelines I follow as well, so I won't name specific locations in this book, except for those sites that are commonly known or have been demolished or repurposed, such as the Lorton Reformatory.

Urban exploration has become very popular over recent years, but it's not a hobby for everyone. Exploring decaying, abandoned buildings can be dangerous. If you do decide to explore abandoned buildings, follow basic safety rules such as doing research on the location, and take all necessary equipment such as flashlights, water, and respirators. Pay attention to your surroundings (including the floors for soft footing or holes, and the ceilings for cave-ins) and if possible, don't explore alone. If you do go alone, alert someone where you'll be. And the biggest rule of all: take nothing but pictures.

In this book is a collection of photographs I've taken over the years as I've explored the state of Virginia. Some of these photos are up to seven years old, and many of these places are no longer around, but still live on through these images, and now this book. I hope you enjoy viewing them almost as much as I did taking them.

1

HISTORY OF VIRGINIA

Virginia, known by its nicknames "the Old Dominion" or the "Mother of Presidents" was one of the original thirteen colonies and has a long, rich, and unique history. Virginia is also sometimes referred to as the "Mother of States" because of its role in being carved into states such as Kentucky and West Virginia, and for the large numbers of American pioneers born in Virginia.

In the early years it was a struggle, but Virginia flourished and survived as a colony thanks to farming, especially tobacco. Over the decades, Virginia's physical and economic landscape changed drastically due to major events such as the Civil War, the Reconstruction Era, and Civil Rights movements. These changes included the invention of the cigarette rolling machine by Albert Bonsack, which made Richmond a hub of new industrial scale production. In 1886, businessman Collis Potter Huntington founded Newport News Shipbuilding, which was responsible for equipping the U.S. Navy with dreadnoughts, battleships, and destroyers.

Urban growth remained sluggish in Virginia after the Civil War as it generally resisted social changes, but several cities in Virginia saw a boom in population. The capital city of Richmond became a national leader in the production of cigarettes, while Danville and Martinsville became more industrialized with a focus on textiles and furniture manufacturing.

In many ways, Virginia still possesses its own divide, and is commonly known as being split between different economic and social regions. These include the sprawling suburban and more industrial, advanced areas of Northern Virginia and the D.C. corridor, the mountainous country/rural areas of Southwest Virginia and the Blue Ridge Mountains, and the eastern Tidewater region.

Throughout the 400-year history since the creation of the Jamestown Colony, major changes and shifts in social and economic stances have left a major impact on the state, especially in the more rural areas. Many schools have been shuttered and left empty. Families have fled their small hometowns, leaving them in "ghost town" status. Local businesses and industries that drove the growth and livelihood of many communities and cities are no longer operational. These homes, businesses, and towns still stand, giving us a glimpse of Virginia's, and America's, past.

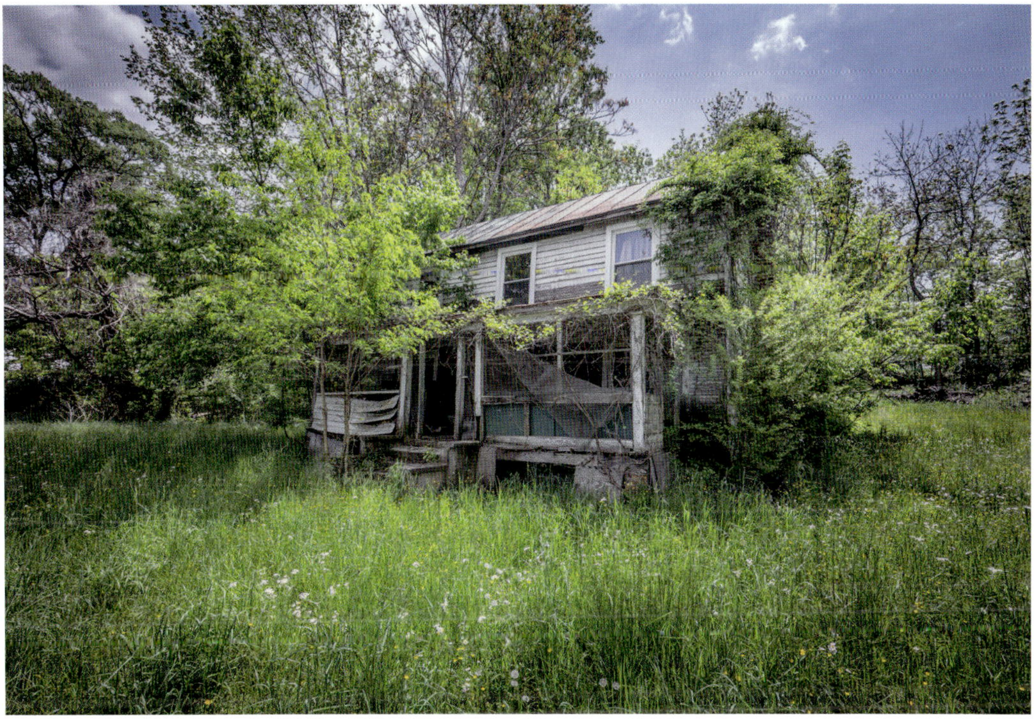

2

ABANDONED HOMES

As farming became less of a viable way to support their families, farmers sold their farms and moved closer to towns and more urban living. In some instances, houses would be left behind after someone passed away, and no one took possession or cared for it over the years. Many times it's a mystery, as historical records have been lost or destroyed over the years, leaving no answer as to why a house has been left abandoned. It's not unheard of to find houses full of furnishings and personal belongings including clothing, military uniforms, toys, and family photo albums. Many of these homes look as if the family just shut the front door one day, to never return.

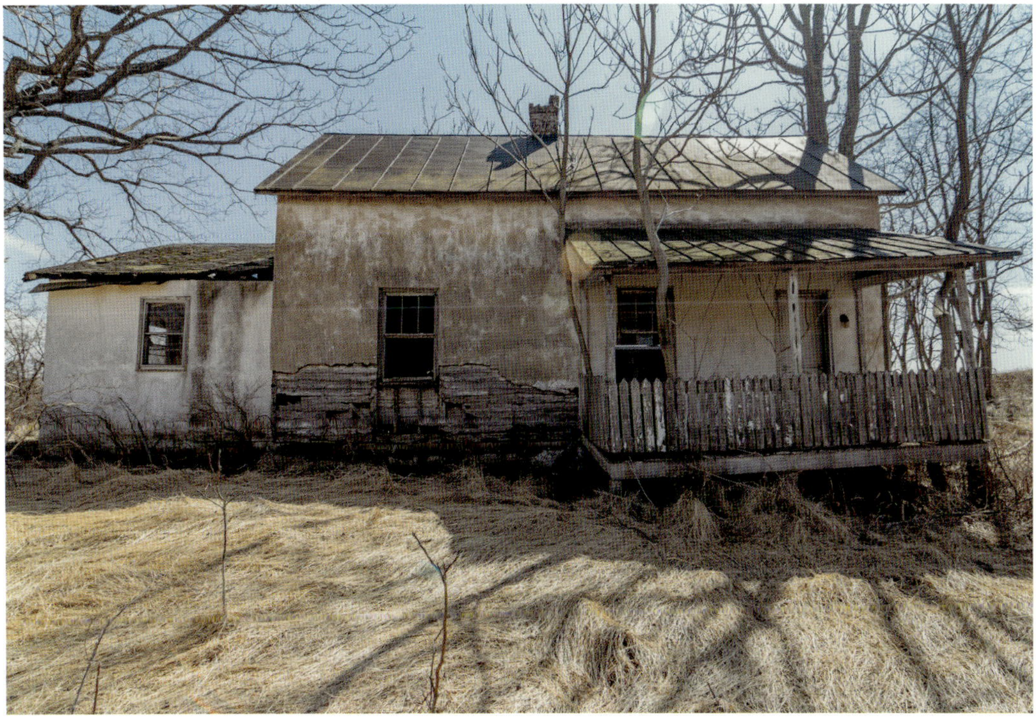

Abandoned Home in Northern Virginia. The porch is slowly starting to detach from the main house.

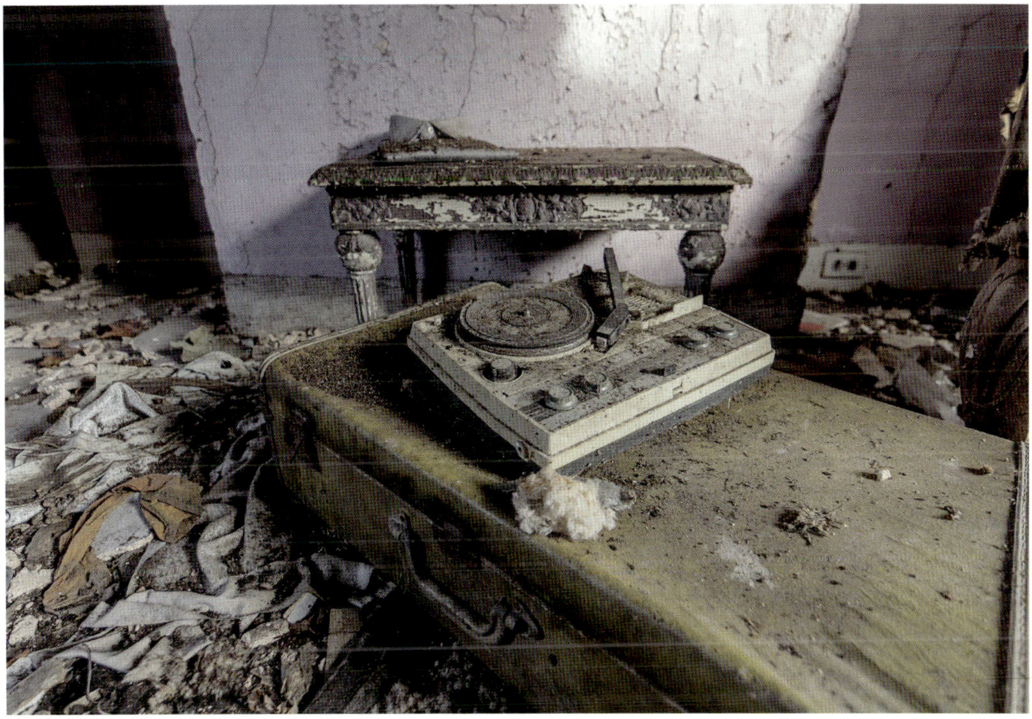

Belongings left behind include a record player, suitcase, and a dress shirt that was never unpinned.

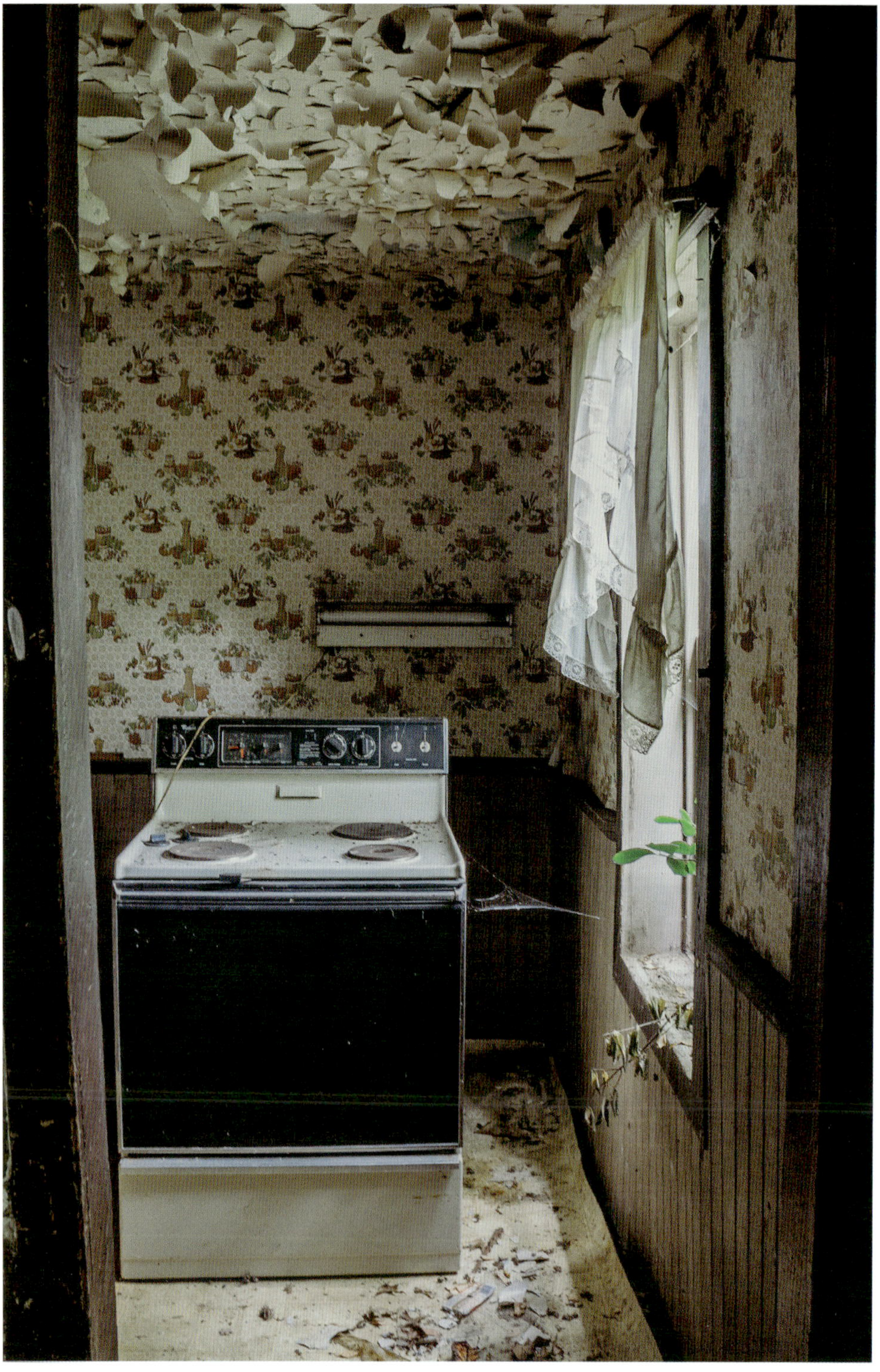

The lead ceiling paint peels away in an abandoned kitchen.

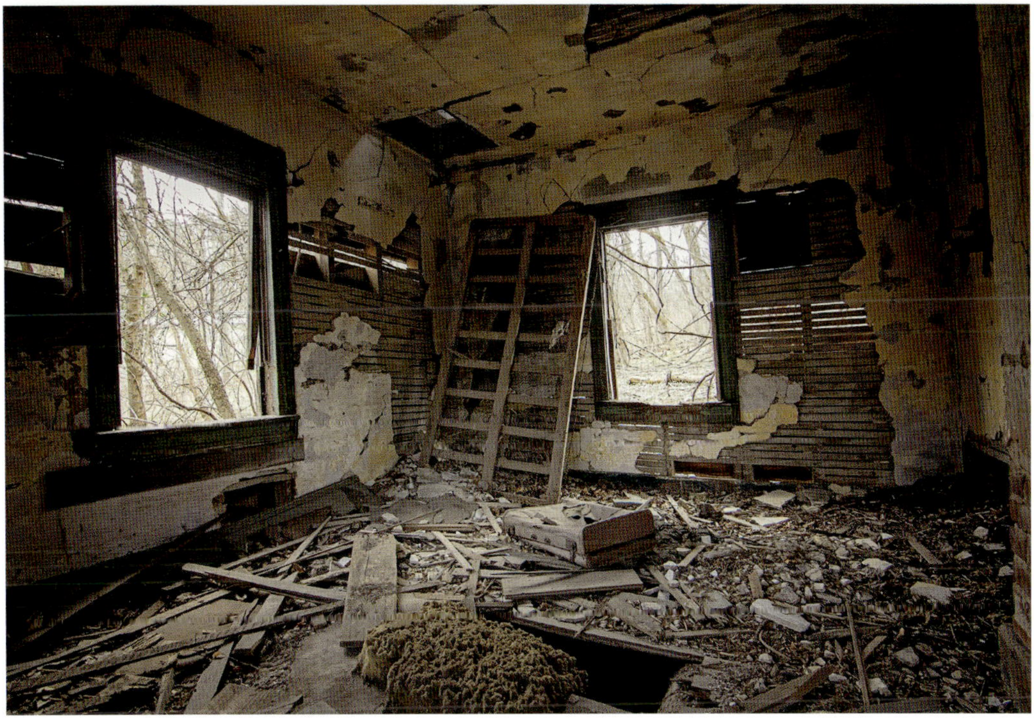

Only a suitcase remains in a second story bedroom.

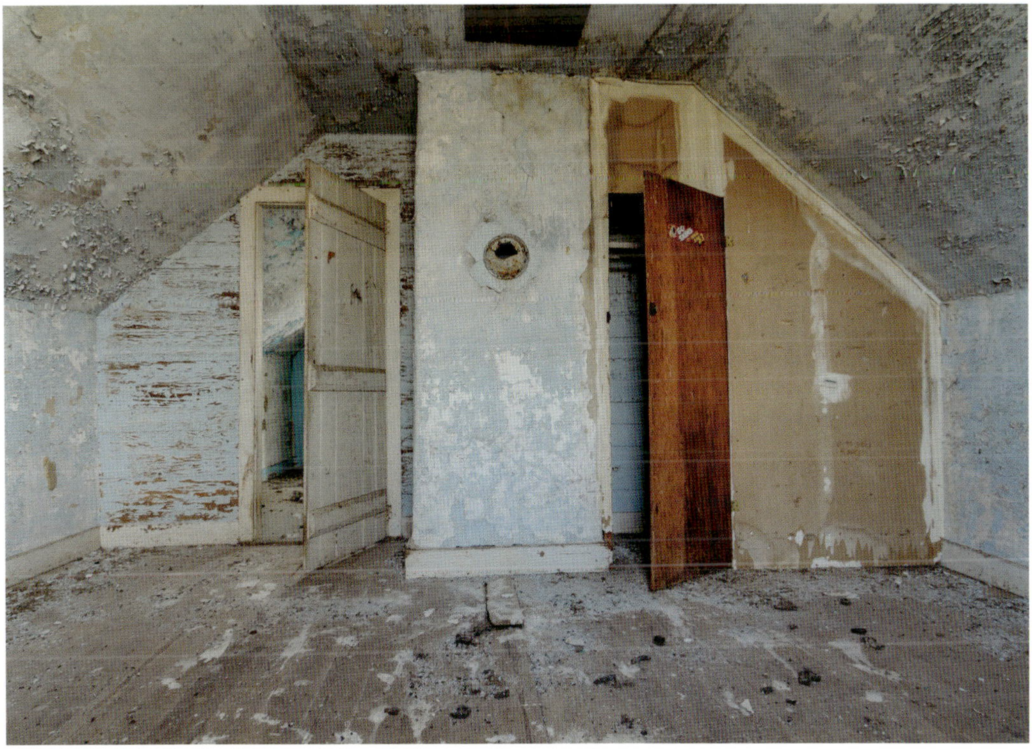

Twin closets in a bedroom.

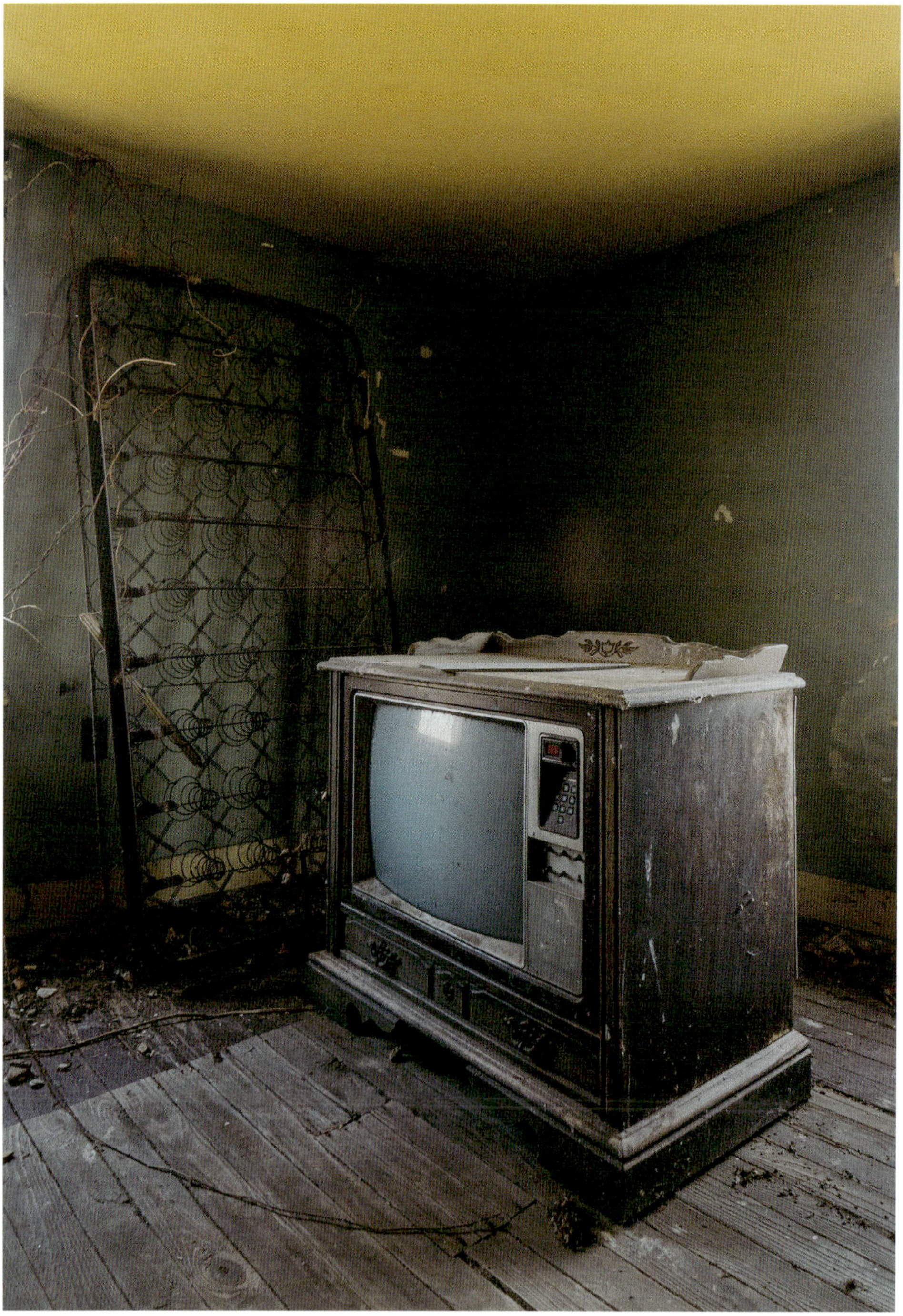

Old console tvs are commonly left behind.

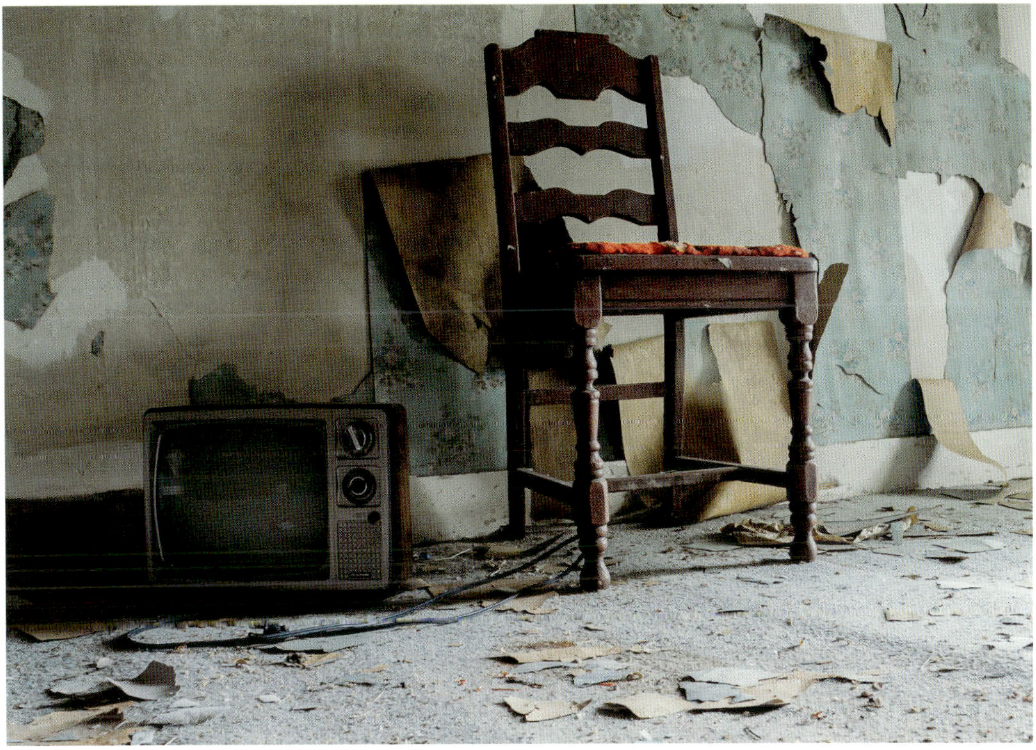

Retro TV and chair in an old home.

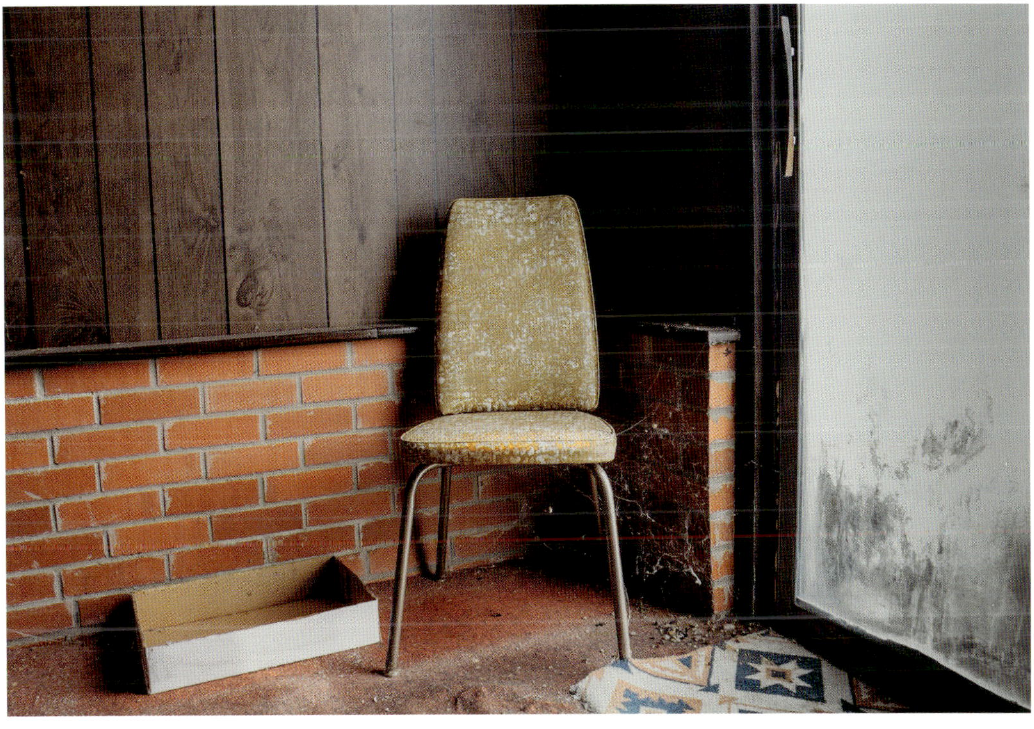

Vintage yellow chair left alone in a 70s style house.

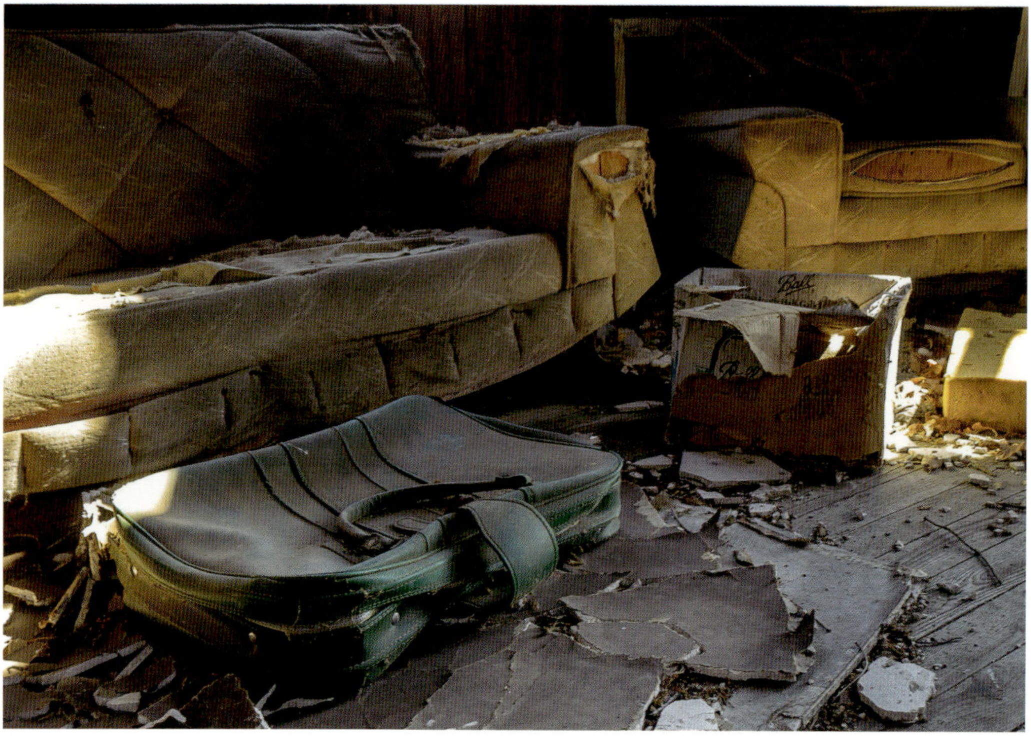

Vintage suitcase left in an old home.

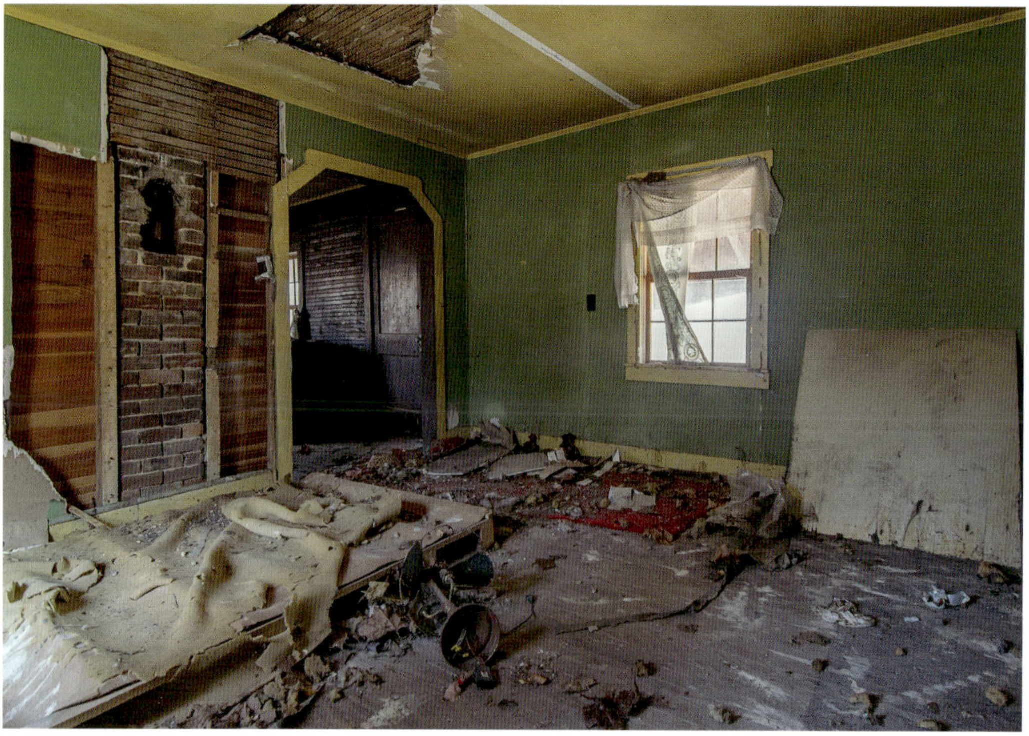

Another home crumbles to pieces after years of decay.

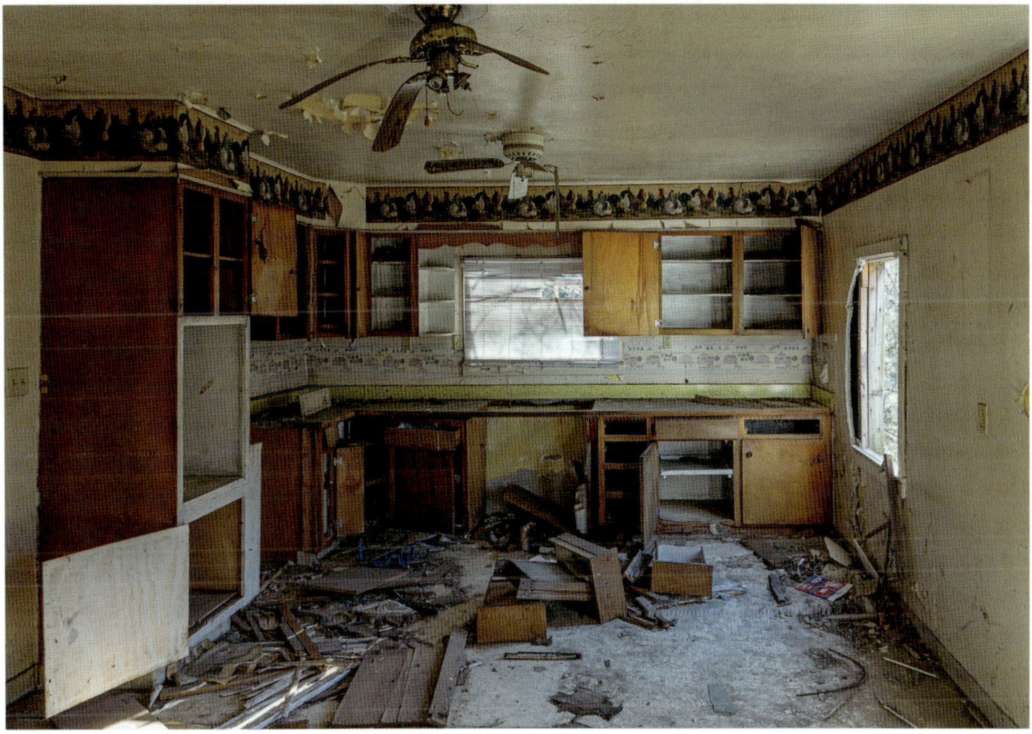

Ransacked kitchen of an abandoned home. The fan blades have warped over the years.

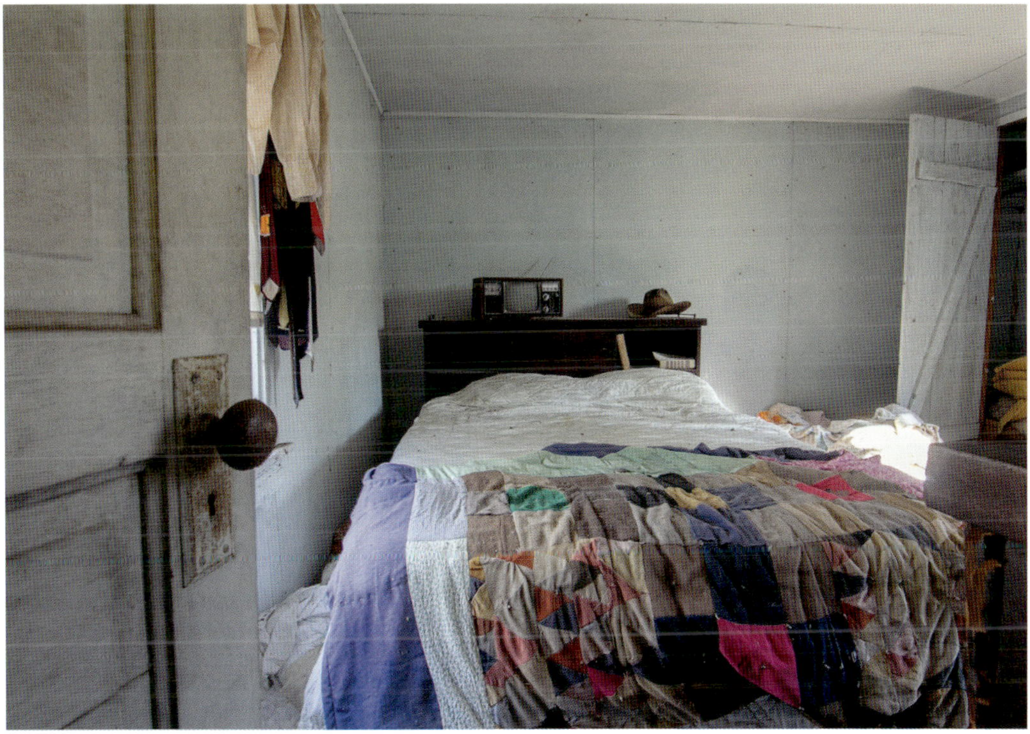

A bed sits made and ready for use in an abandoned home.

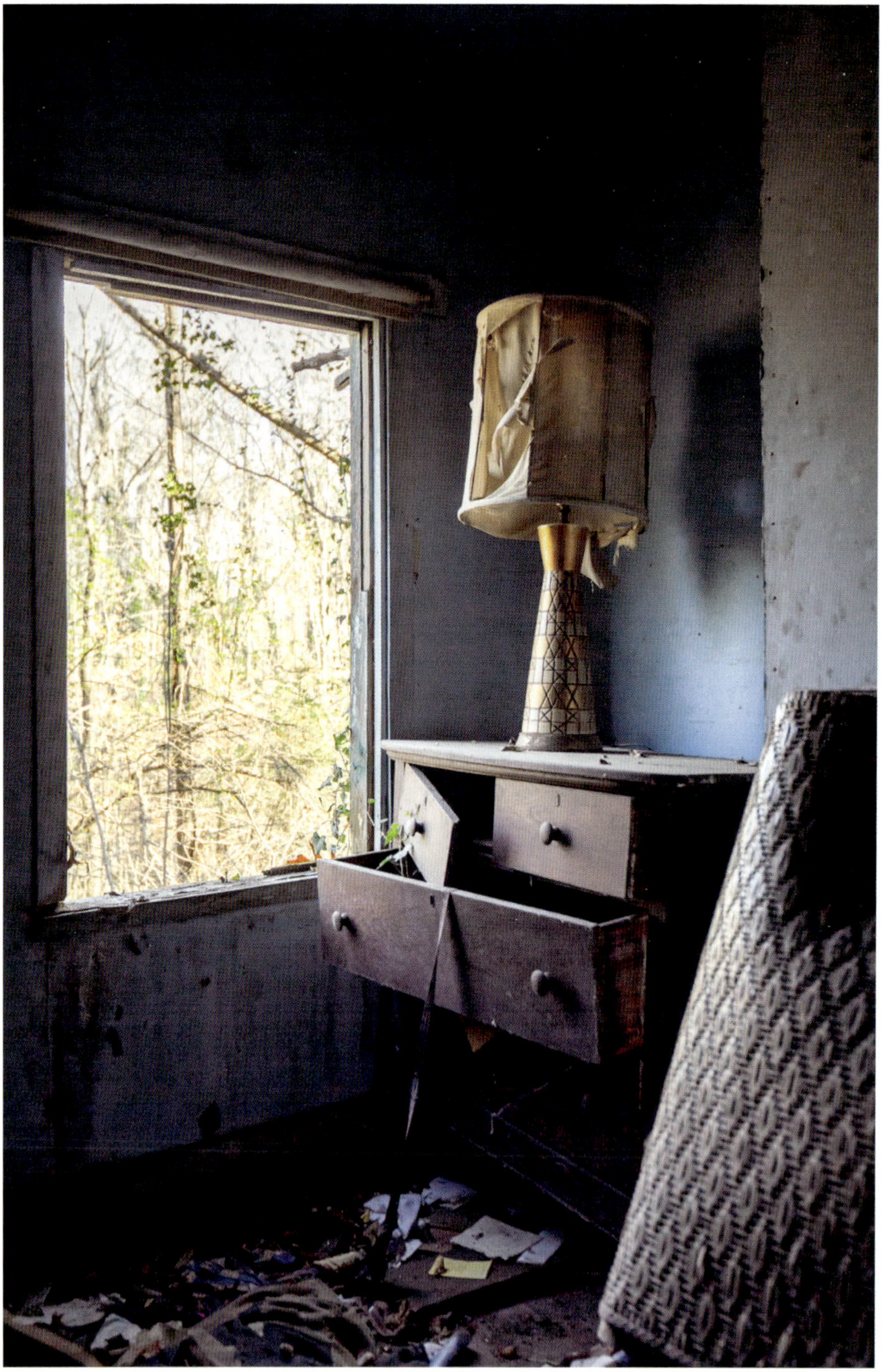

Bedside lamp beside a broken bedroom window.

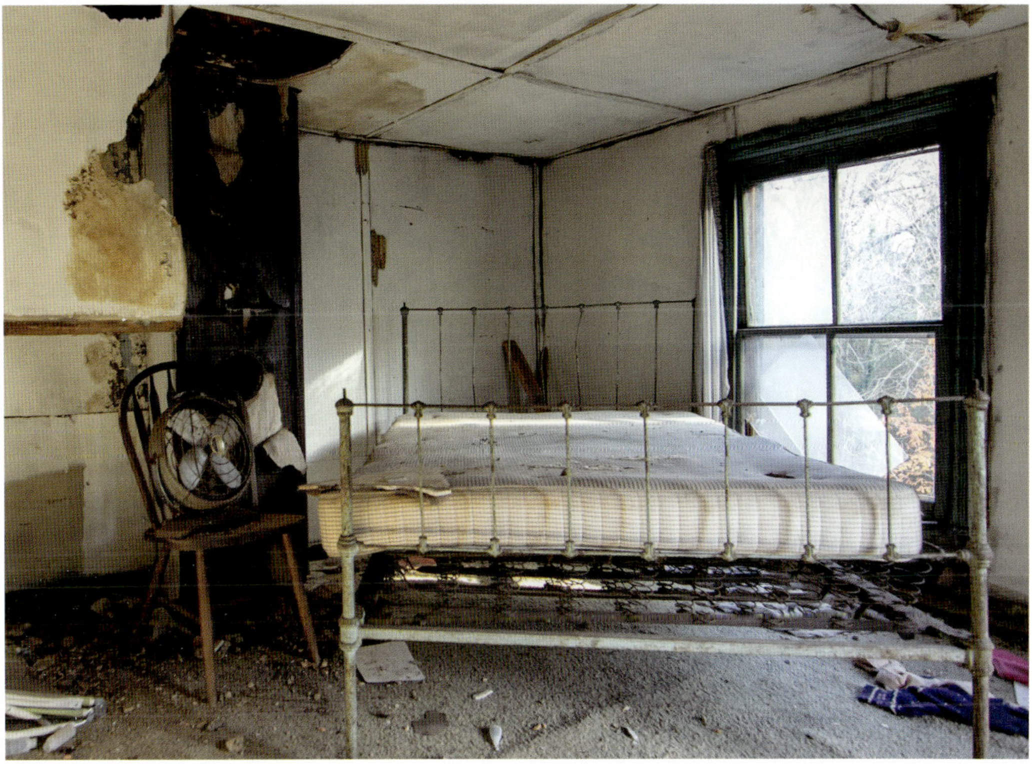

Bed frame left behind in an old home.

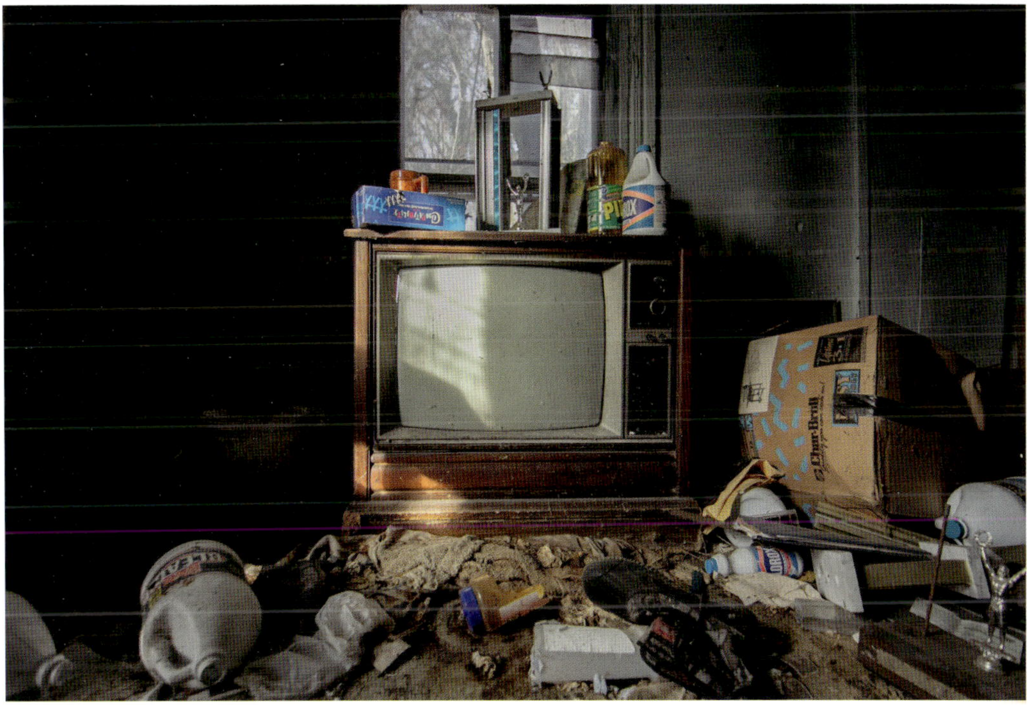

Broken trophies littered the floors of this abandoned home

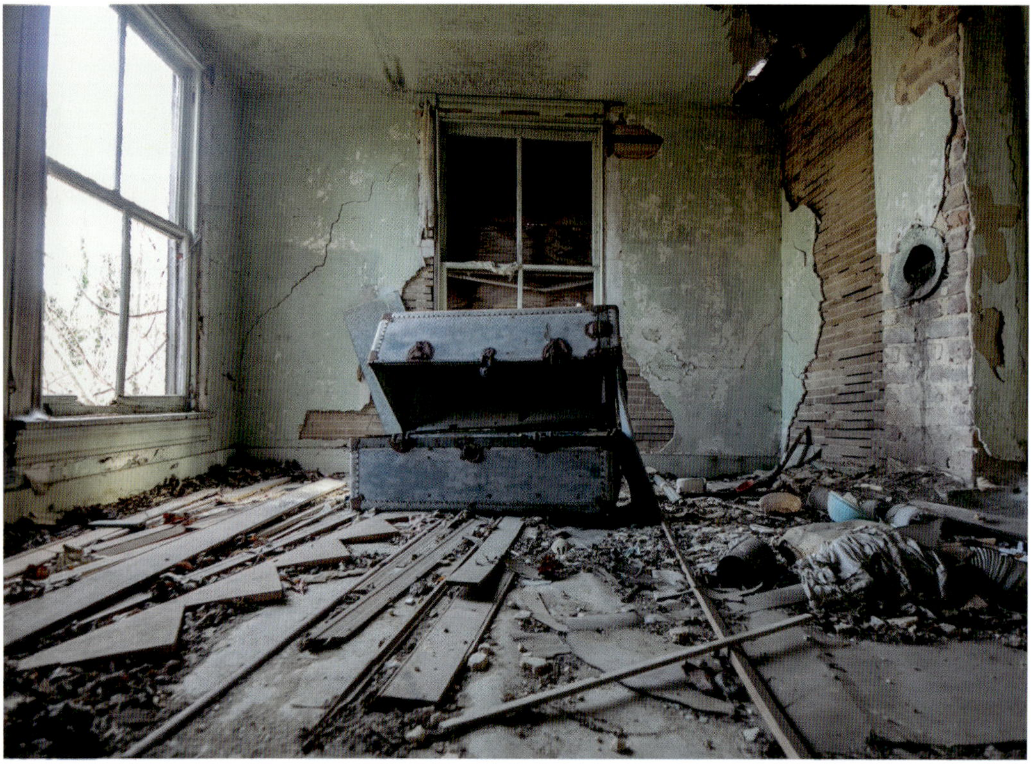

Empty trunk ready to be packed.

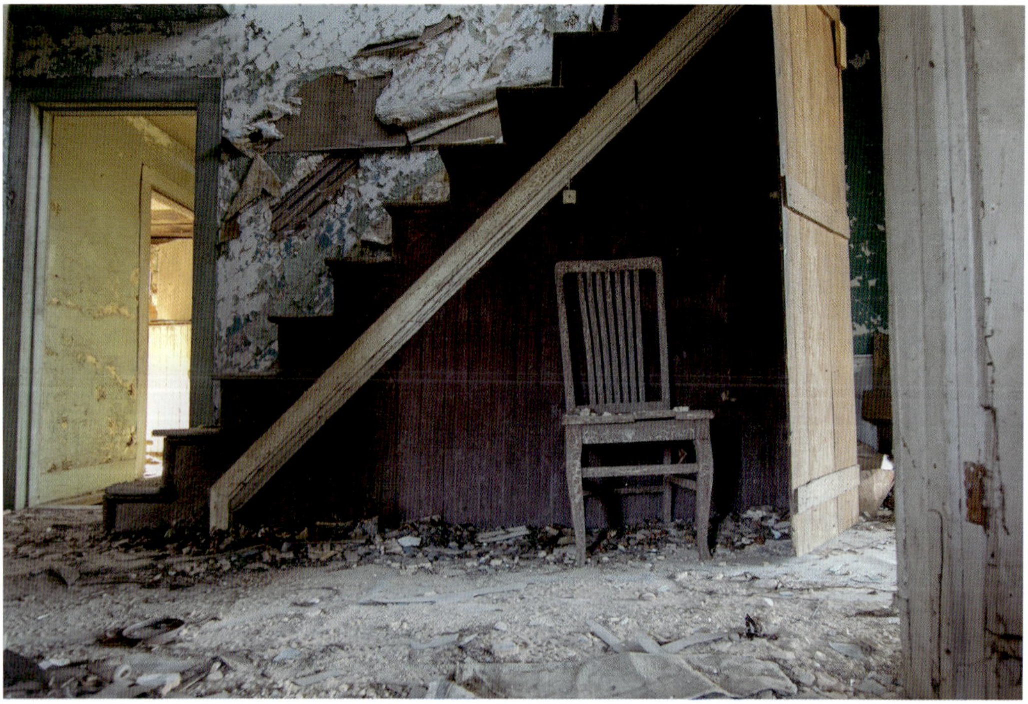

Lone chair in the entryway of a country home.

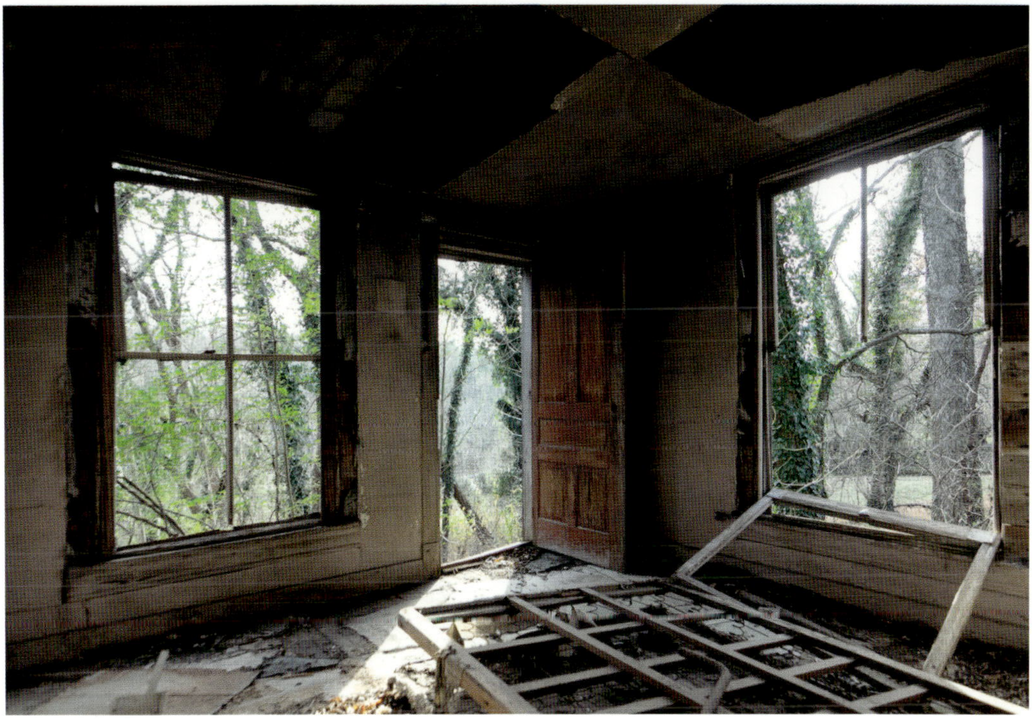

Windows missing from a bedroom.

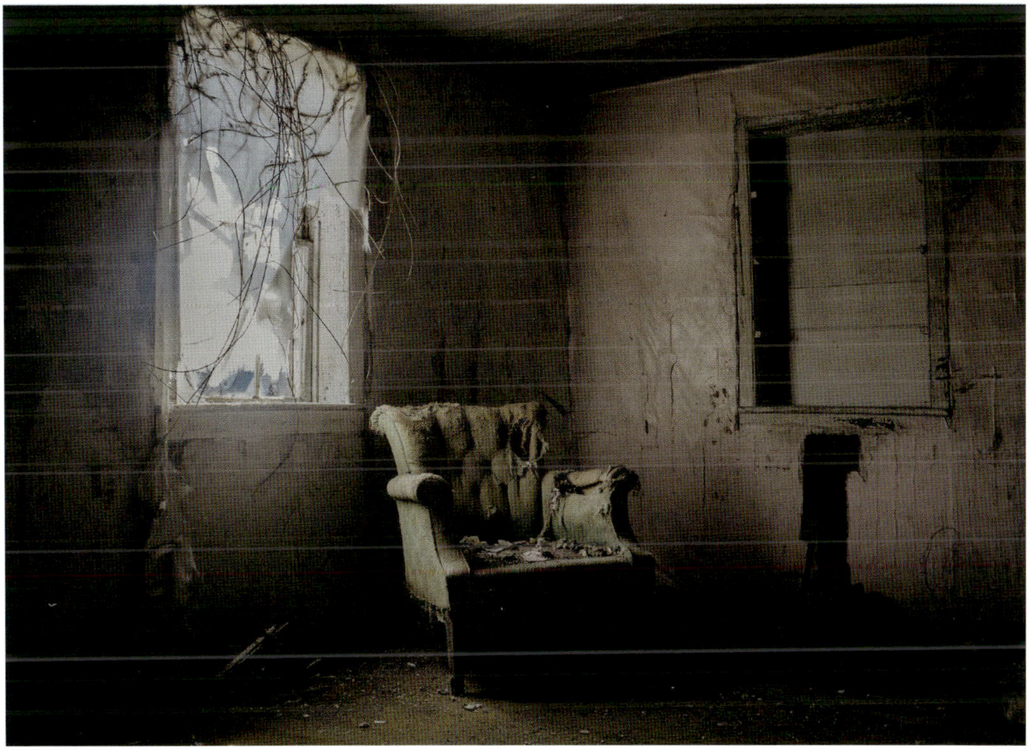

Valuable vintage style furniture left behind in old homes to rot away.

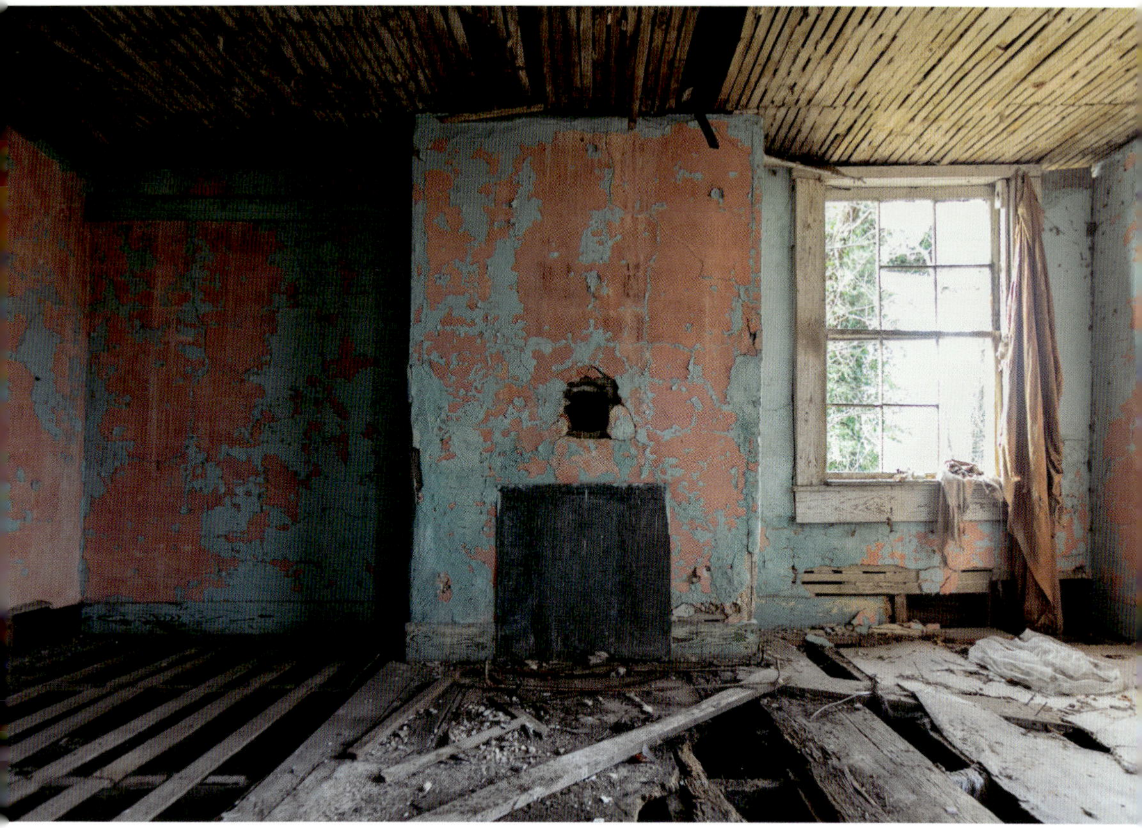

Only a few planks remain in this bedroom.

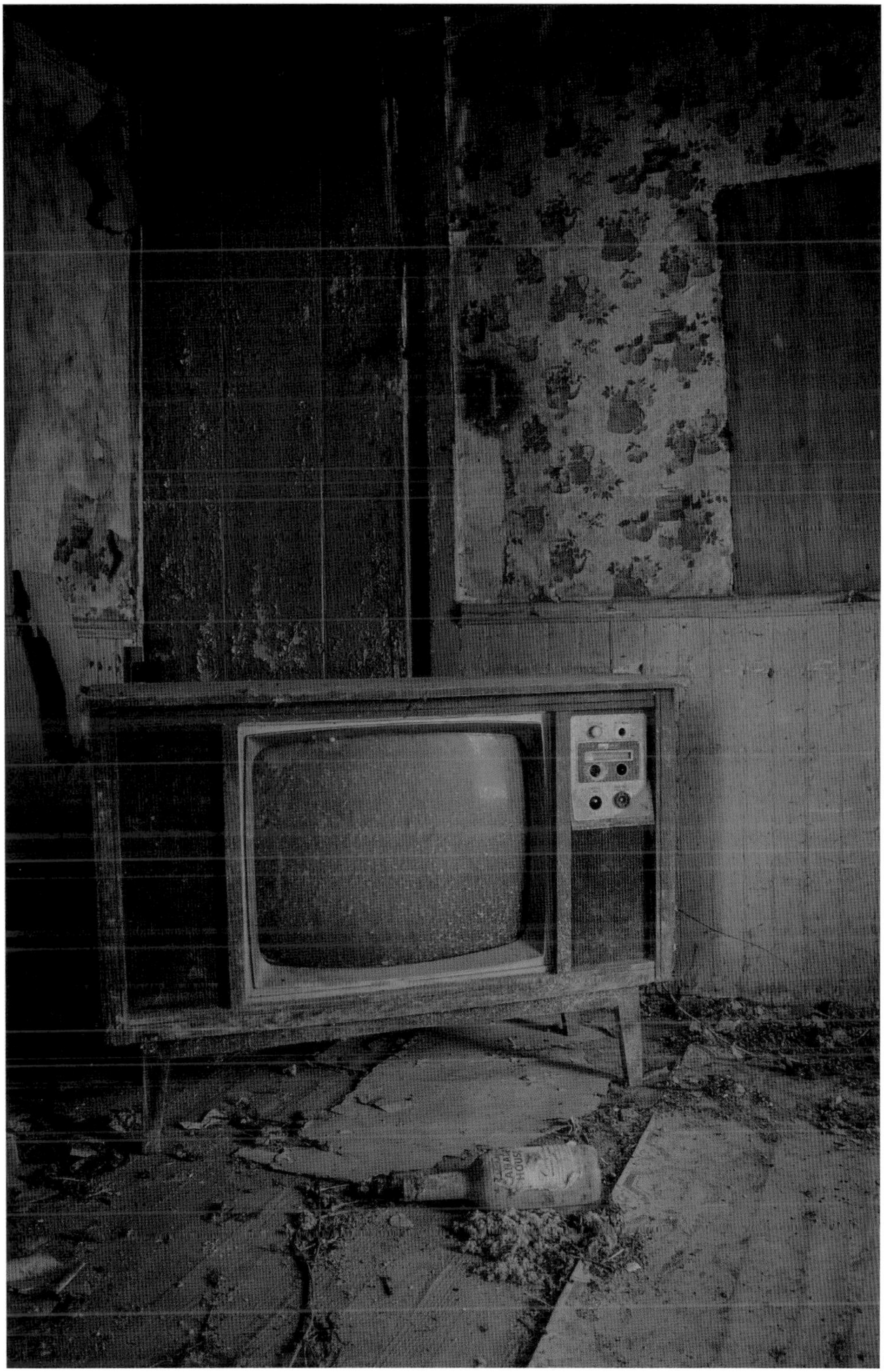

Another old tv left behind in the family room.

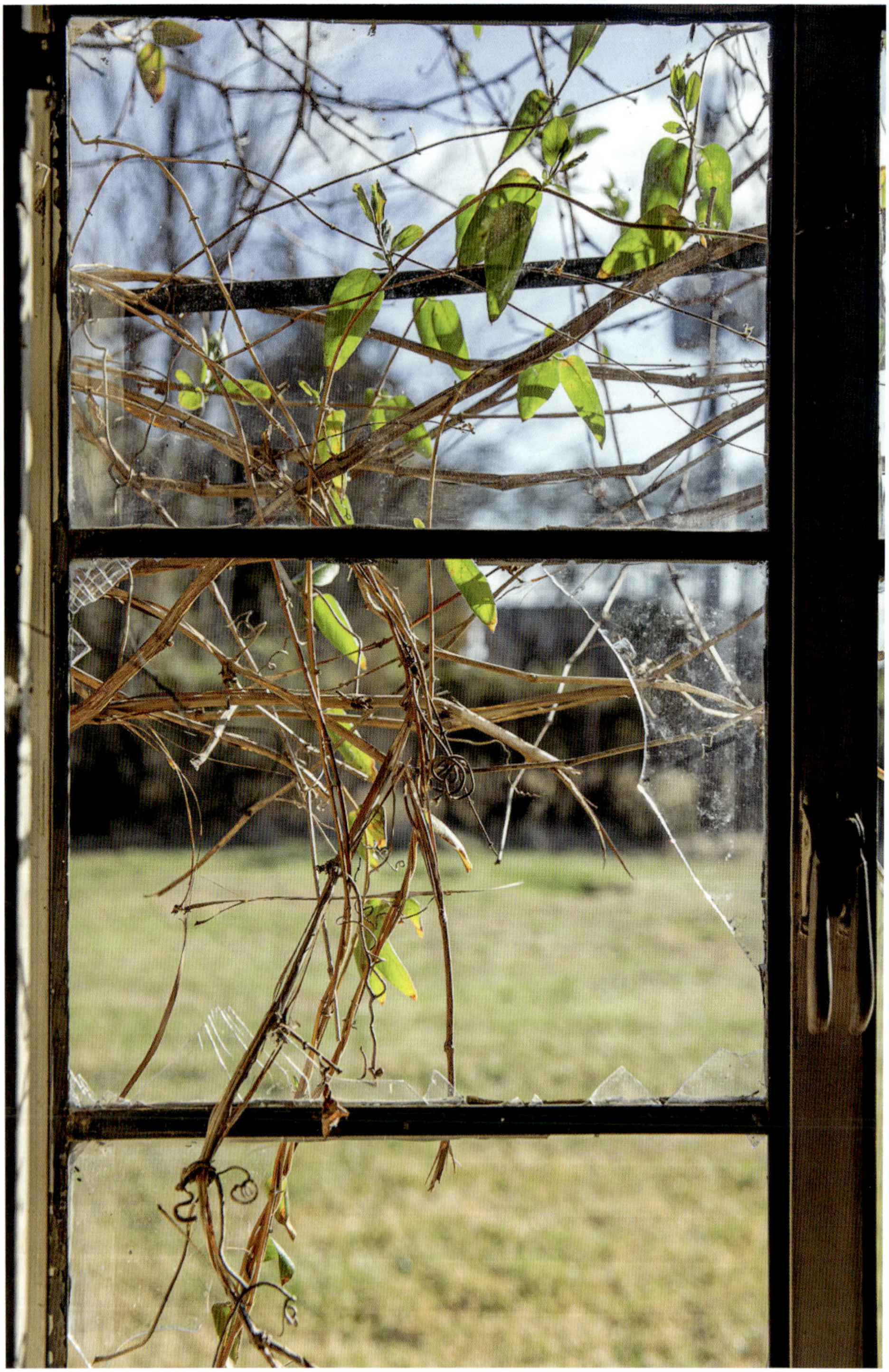

Plant vines growing through a broken window.

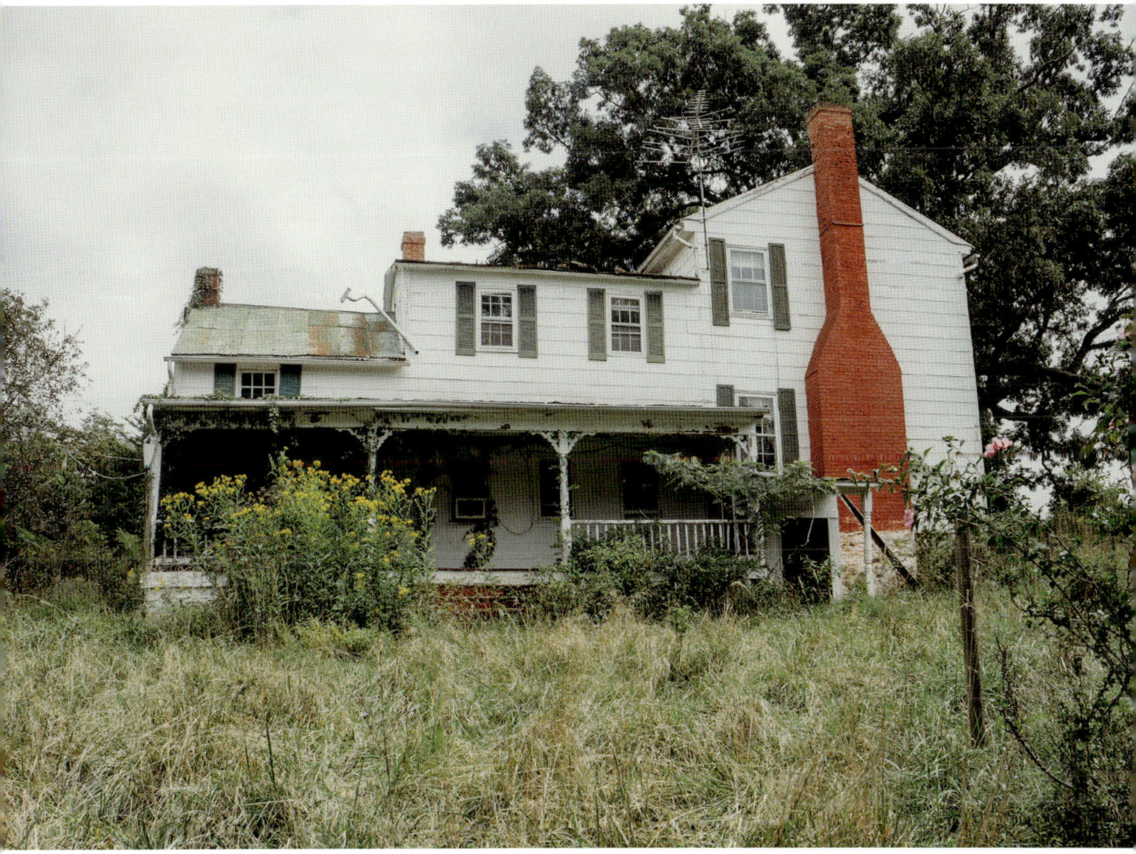

An old farmhouse being taken over by vines.

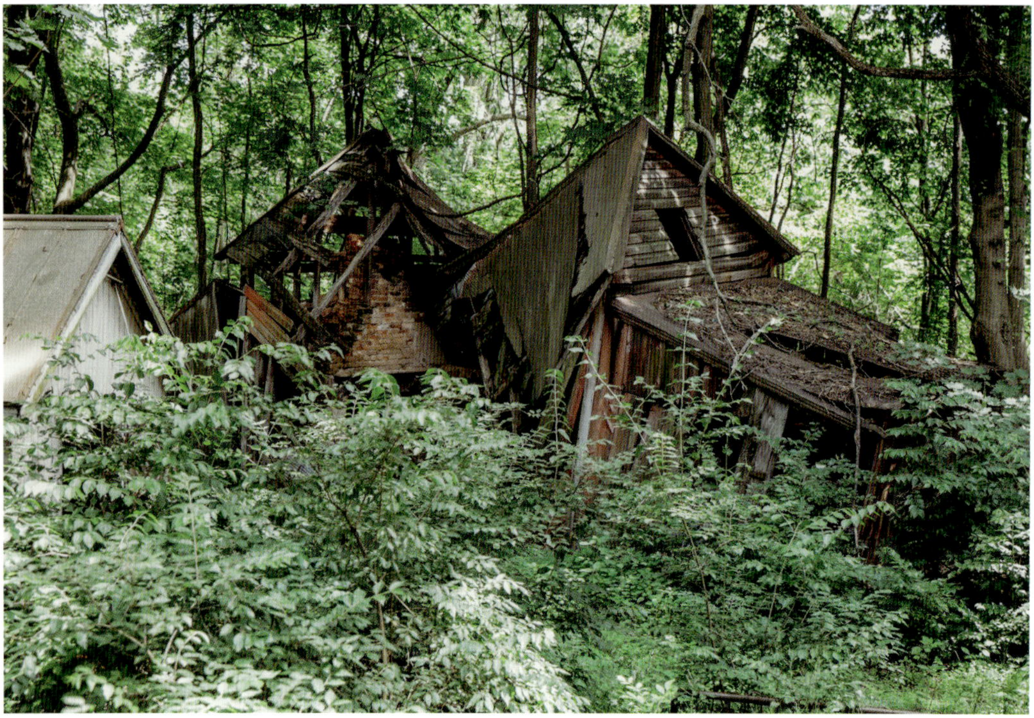

An abandoned home slowly collapses and fades back into the ground.

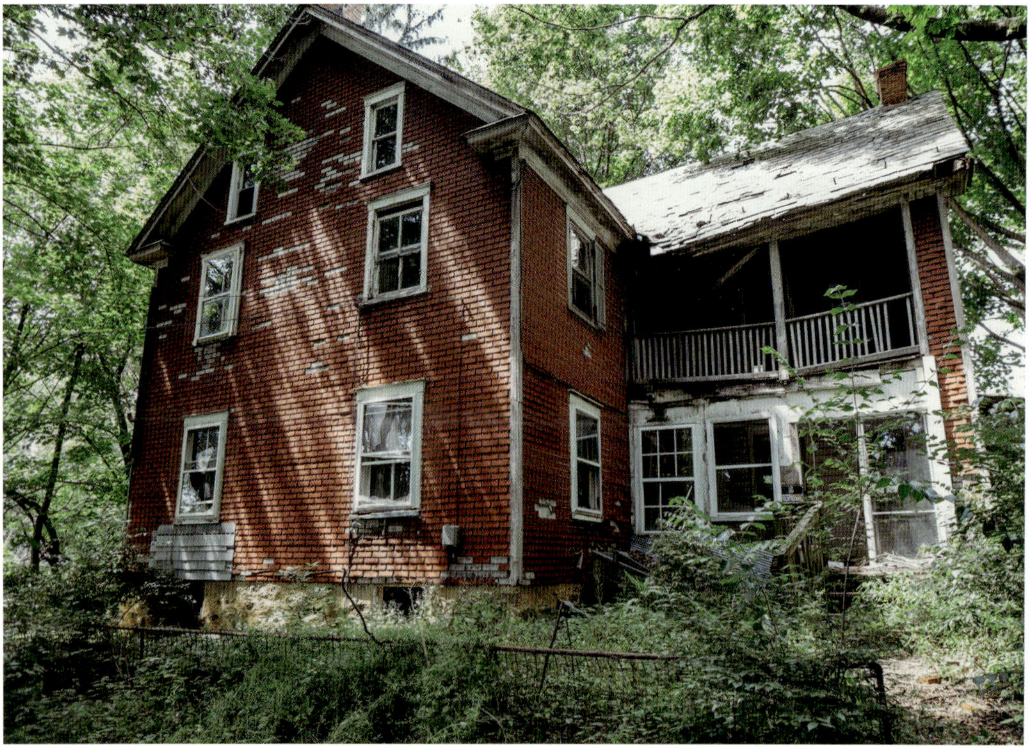

An old brick house remains hidden among the trees in Virginia.

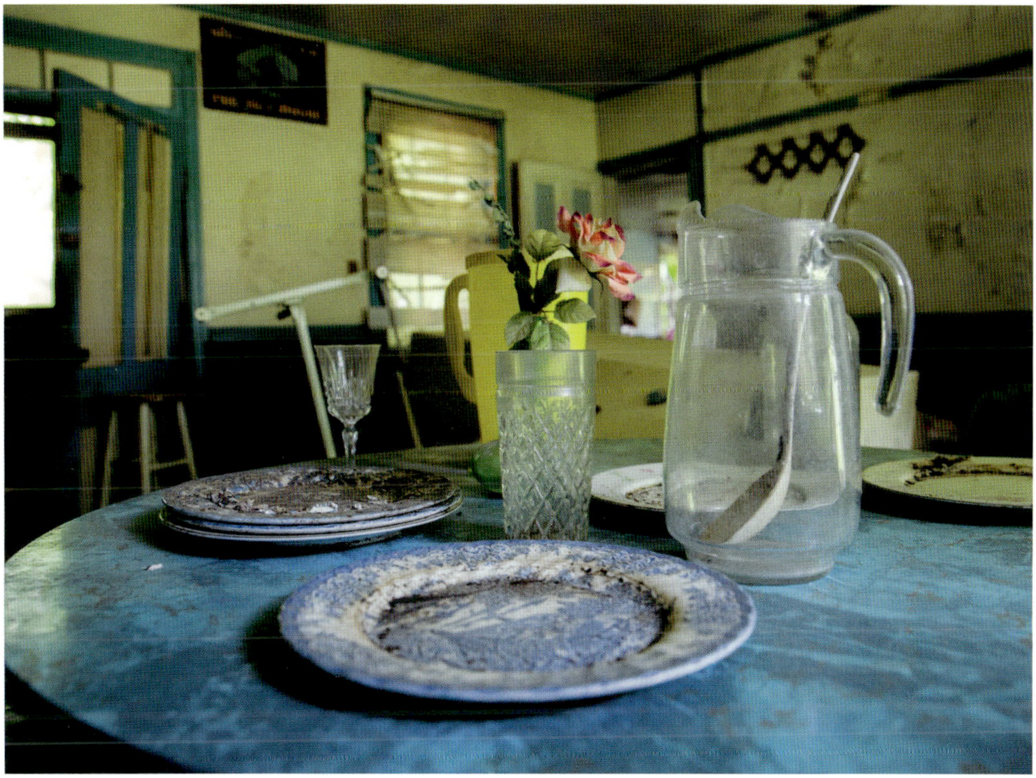

The table is still set in this abandoned kitchen.

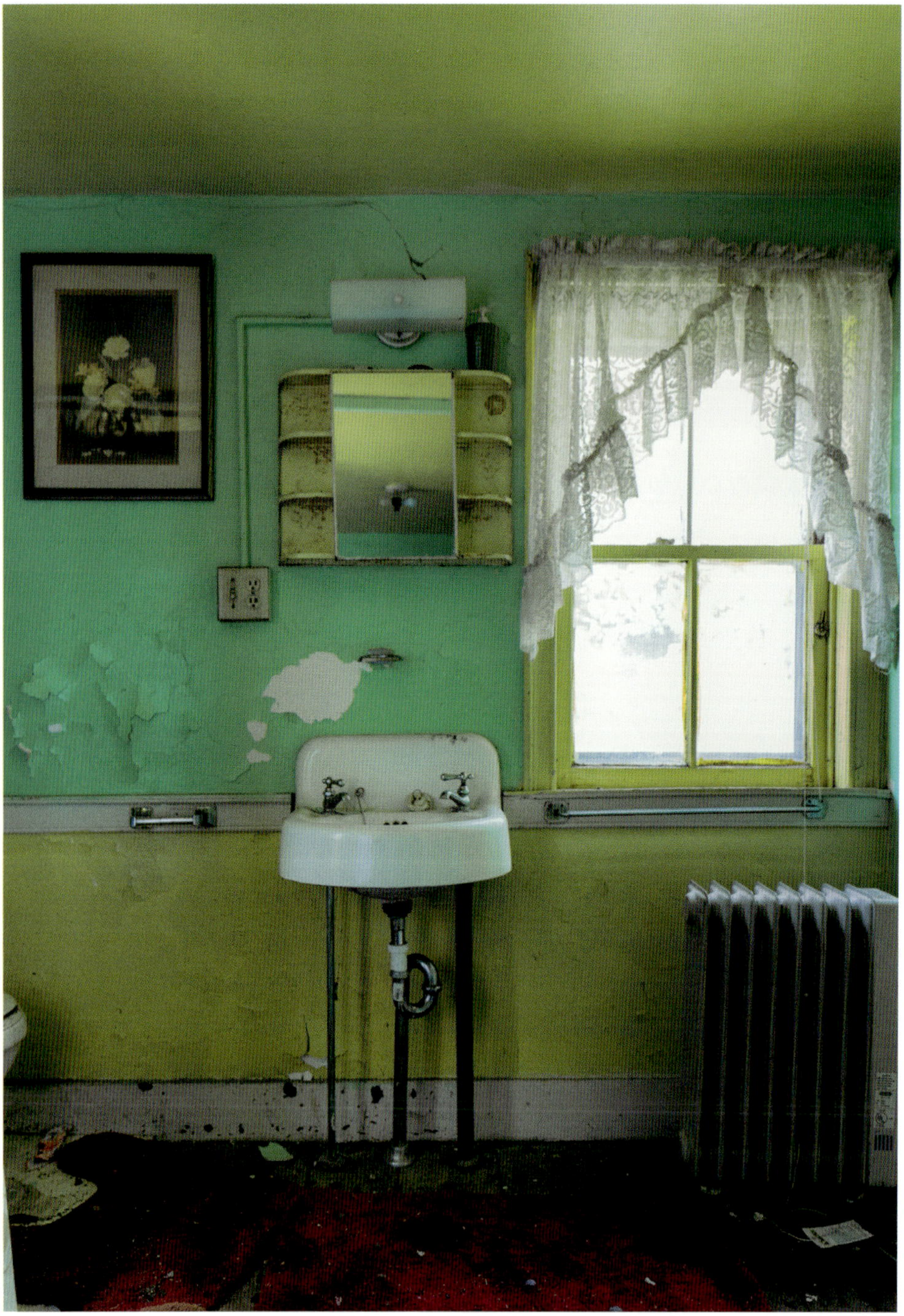

Vintage sink and bright green and yellow bathroom walls.

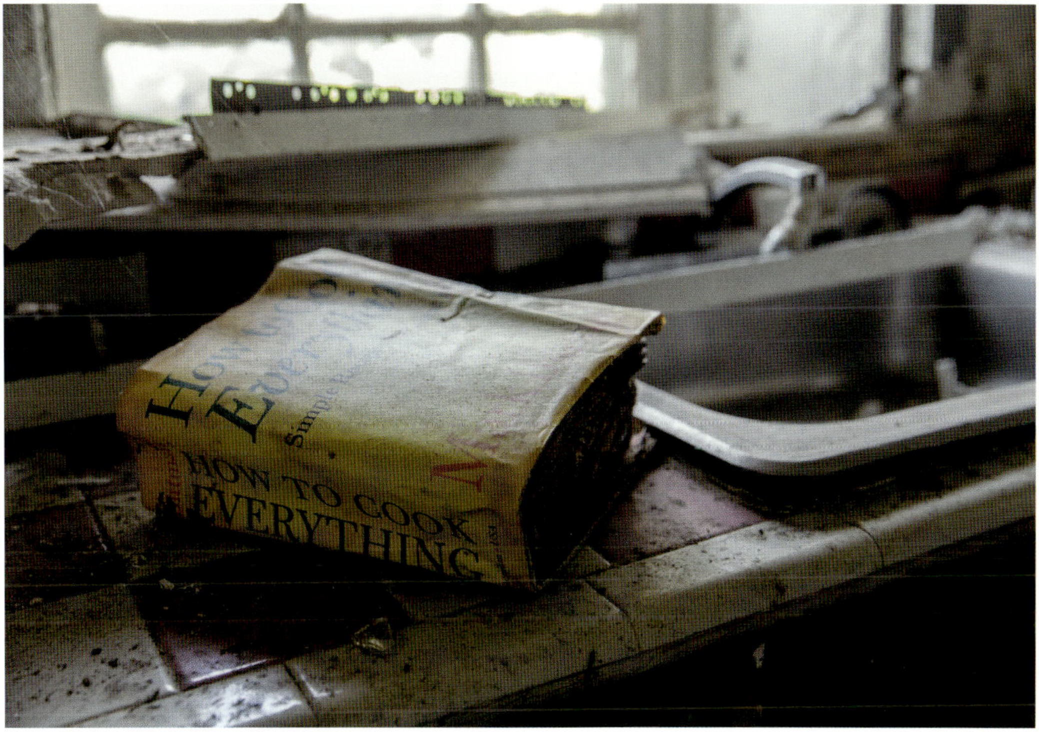

How to Cook Everything. A staple of the kitchen.

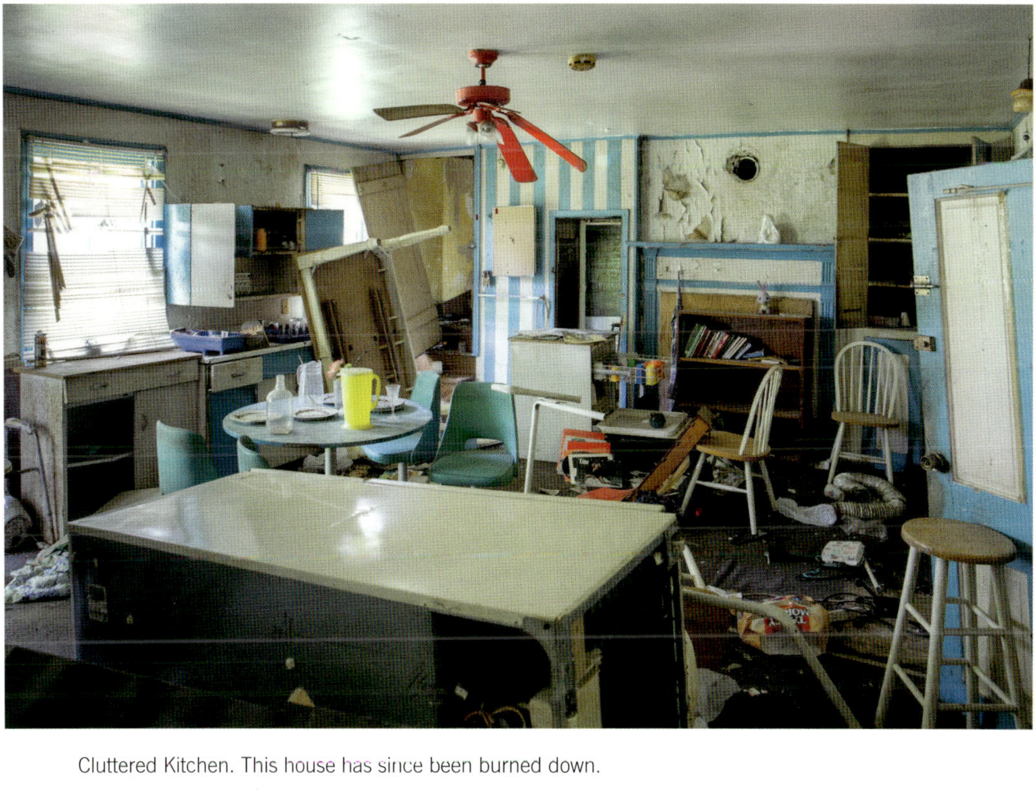

Cluttered Kitchen. This house has since been burned down.

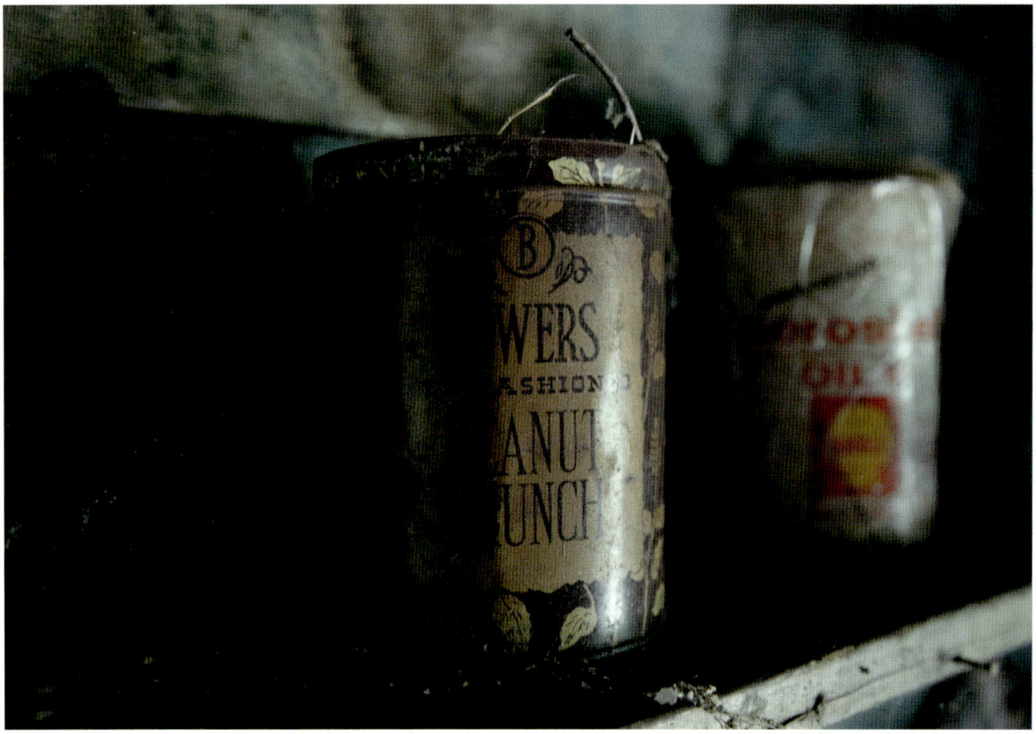

Many houses still have shelves filled with canned goods, such as this jar of peanut butter.

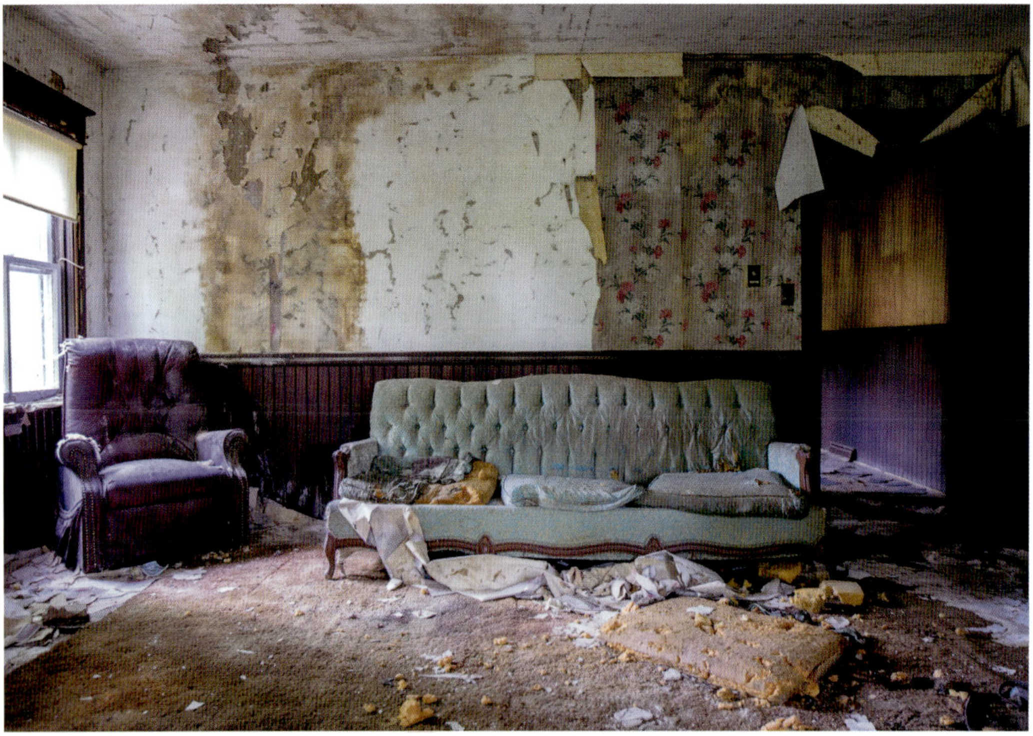

Sitting room in an abandoned home.

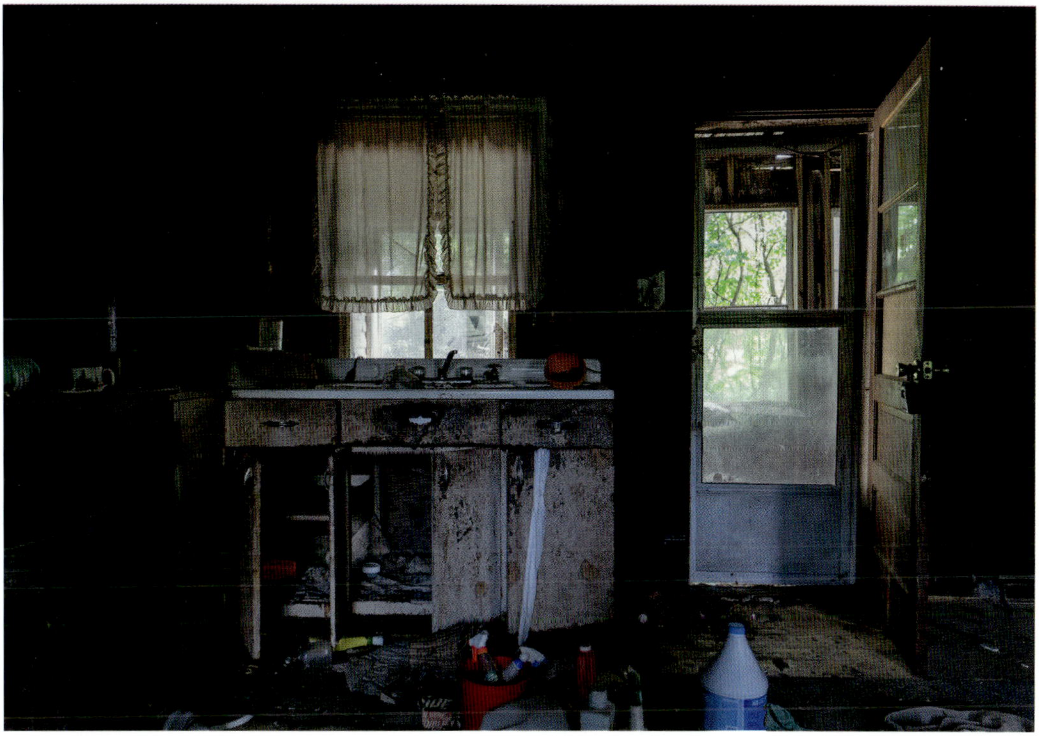

A bucket of cleaning supplies sit ready to use in a decaying kitchen.

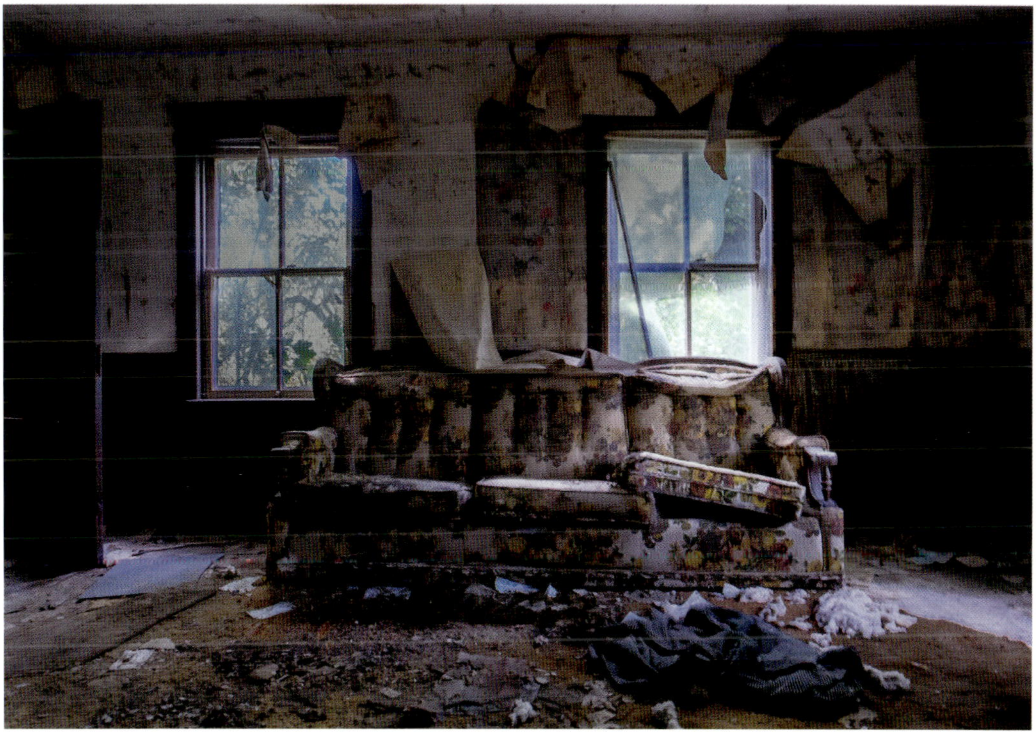

The walls slowly fall apart around the living room couch.

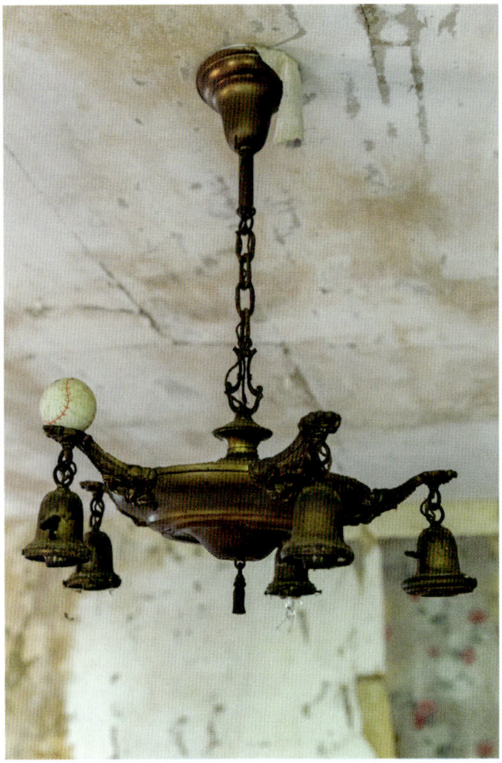

Antique chandelier in the living room.

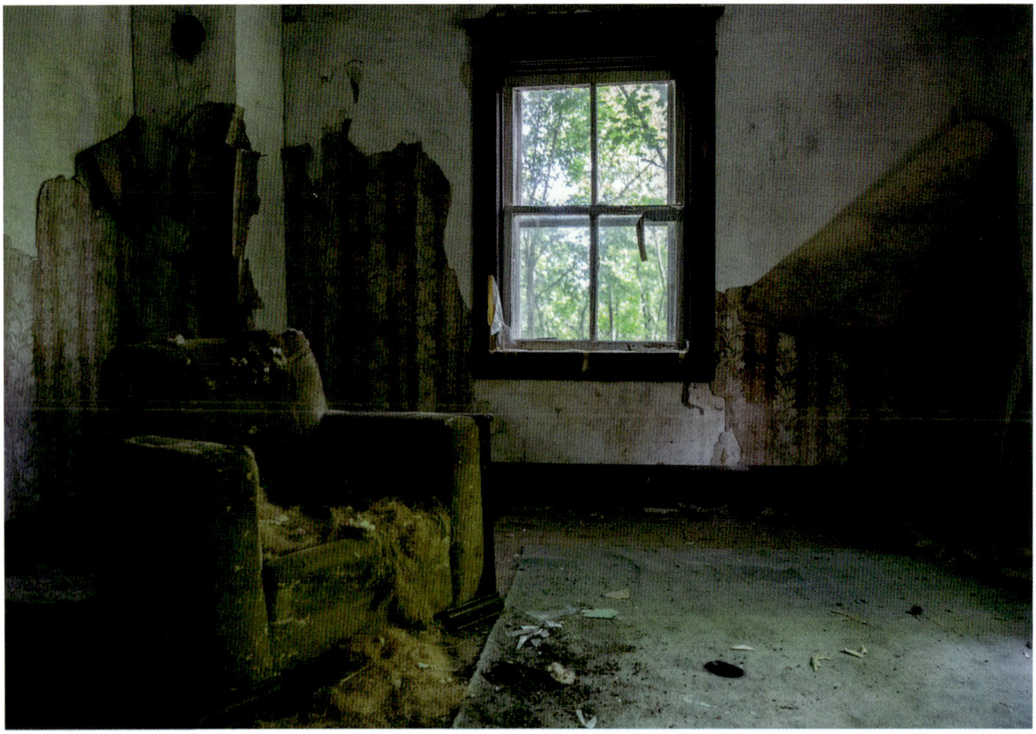

A lone chair in an upstairs bedroom.

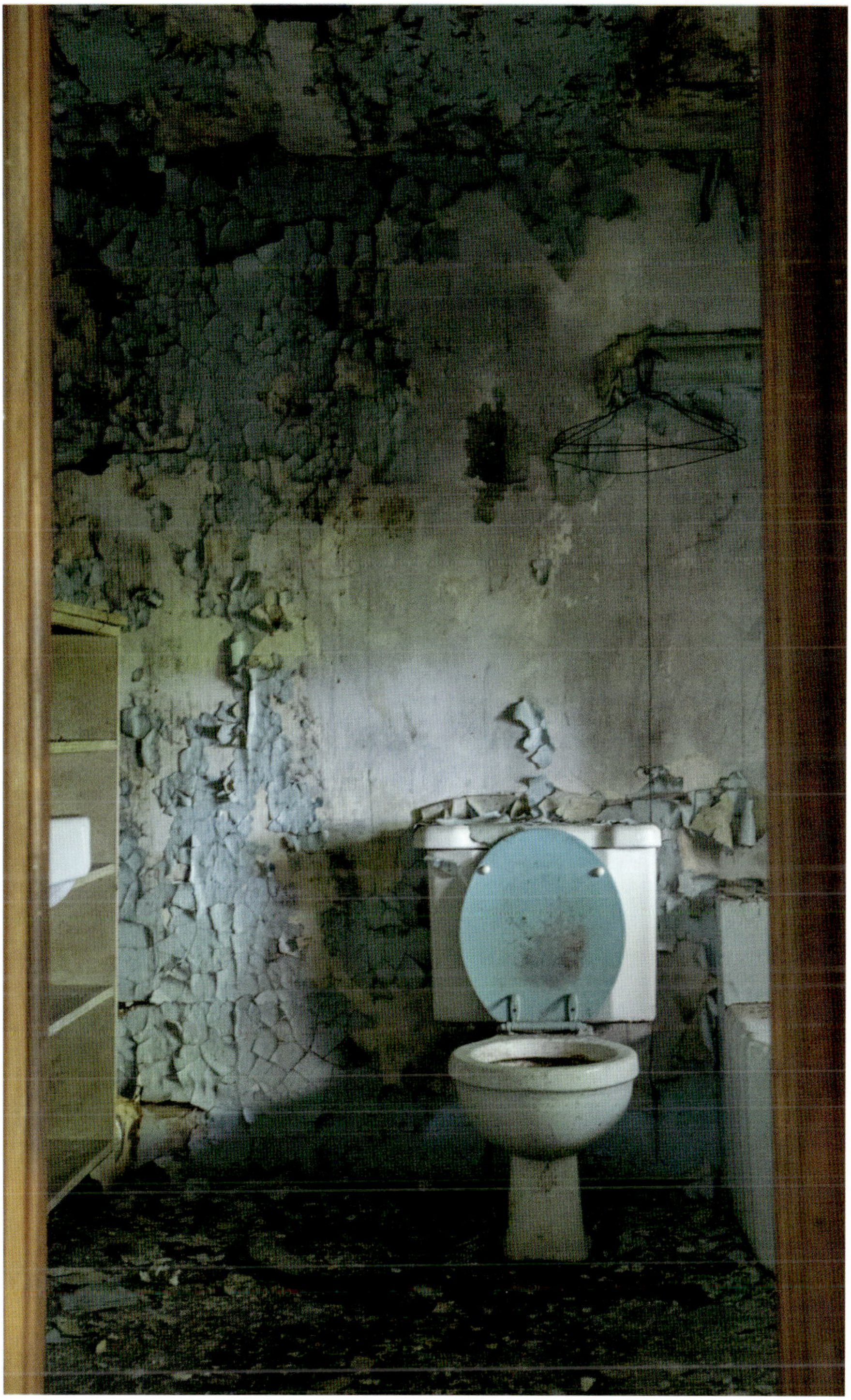

Paint peels off the bathroom walls.

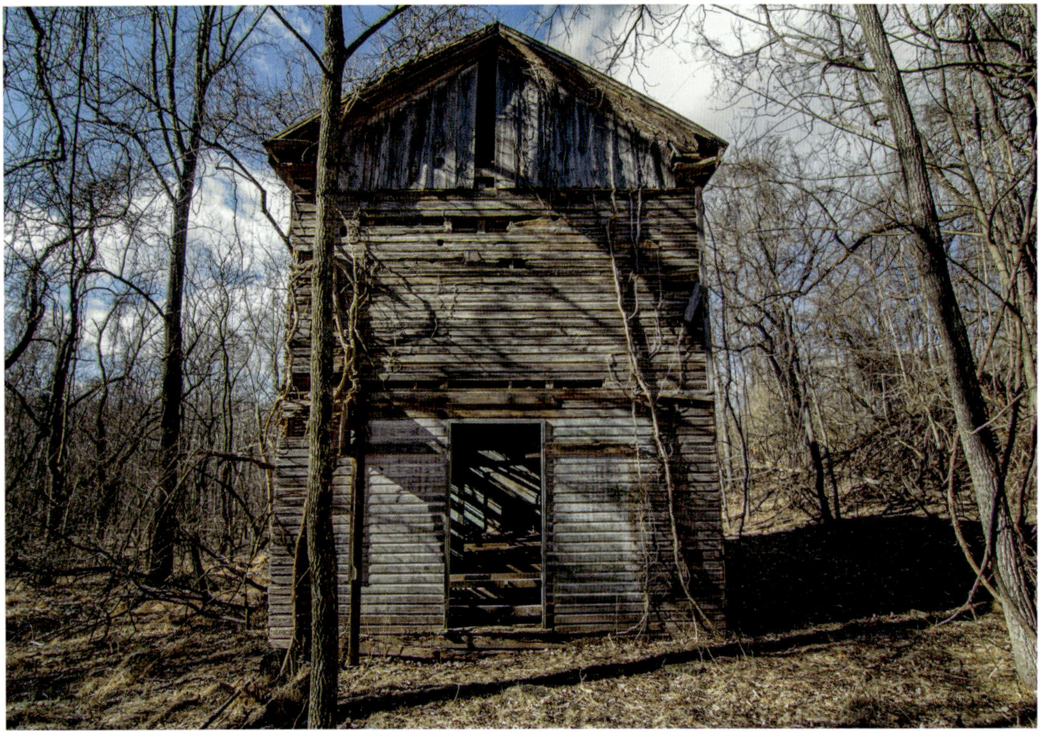

The shell of a home stands by itself in the middle of the woods.

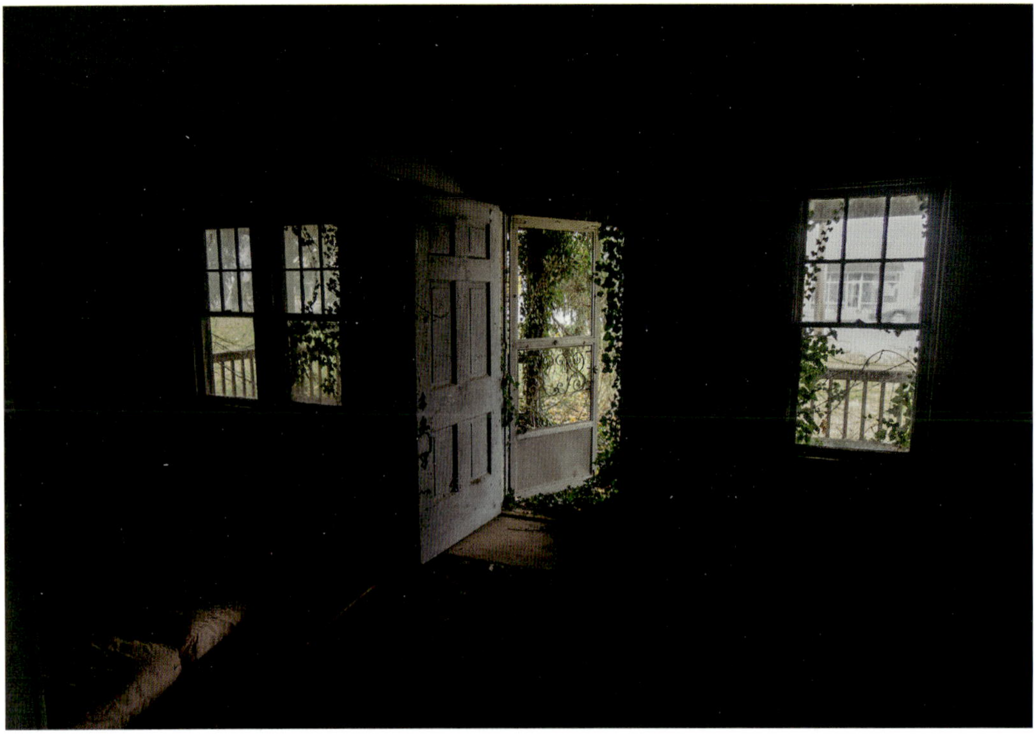

A small home being devoured by vines, with signs of squatters.

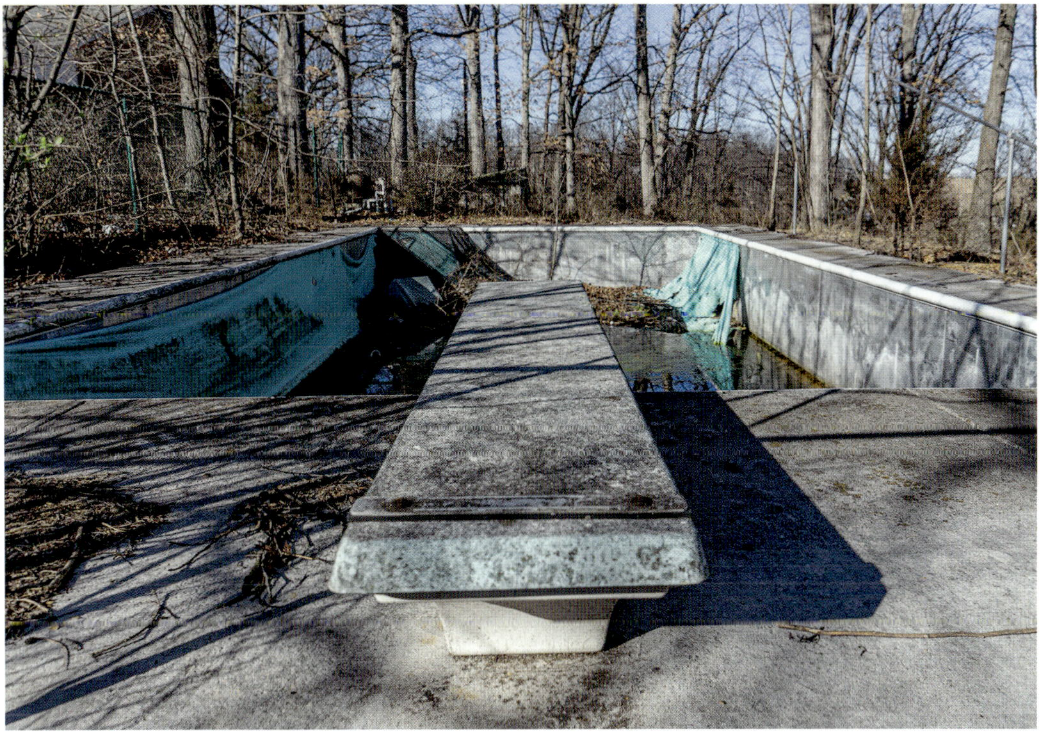

Swimming pools are left to fill with rain water and debris.

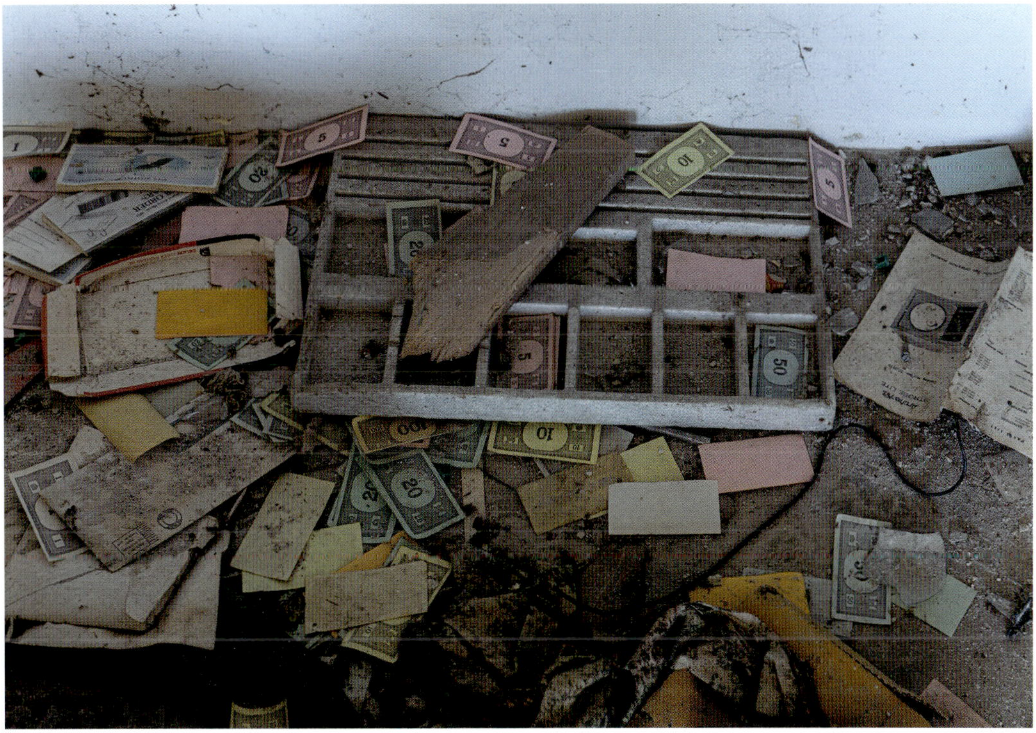

A game of Monopoly left behind in a child's bedroom.

3

VIRGINIA'S ABANDONED SCHOOLS

EASTERN SHORE SCHOOL

This high school opened in 1932 to serve what is still one of the poorest counties in the state. The graduation of the last high school students happened in 1984, but the school continued to function as a middle school until it finally closed in 2005. In 2011, it was listed on the National Register of Historic Places of Virginia.

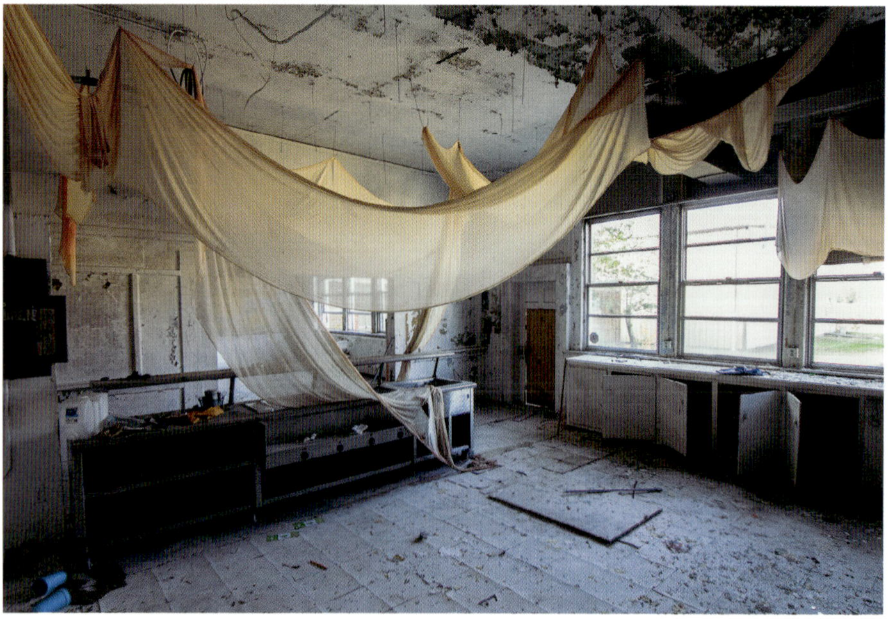

The kitchen in an abandoned school was once used for an art installation.

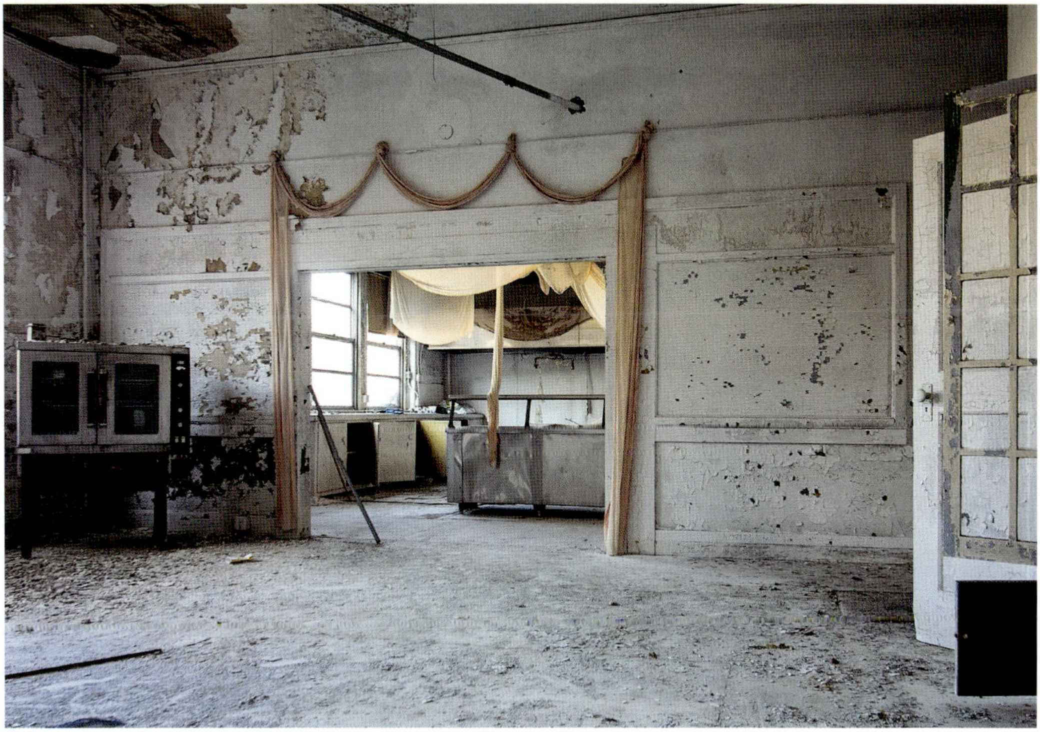

The school kitchen.

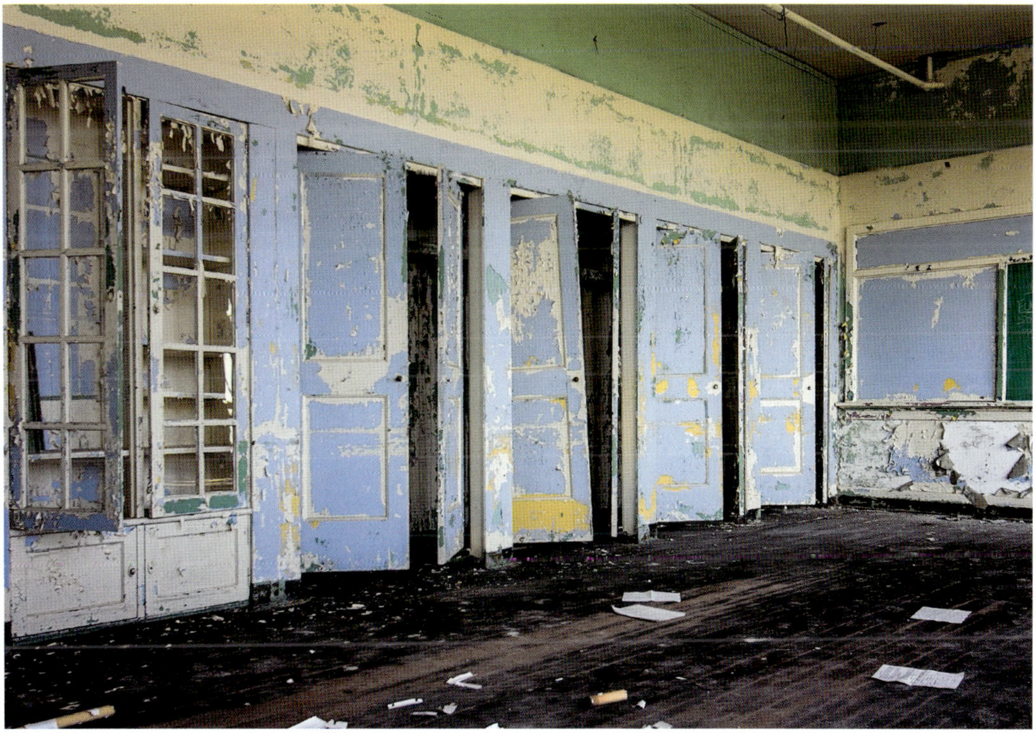

Cabinets losing their paint in an old classroom.

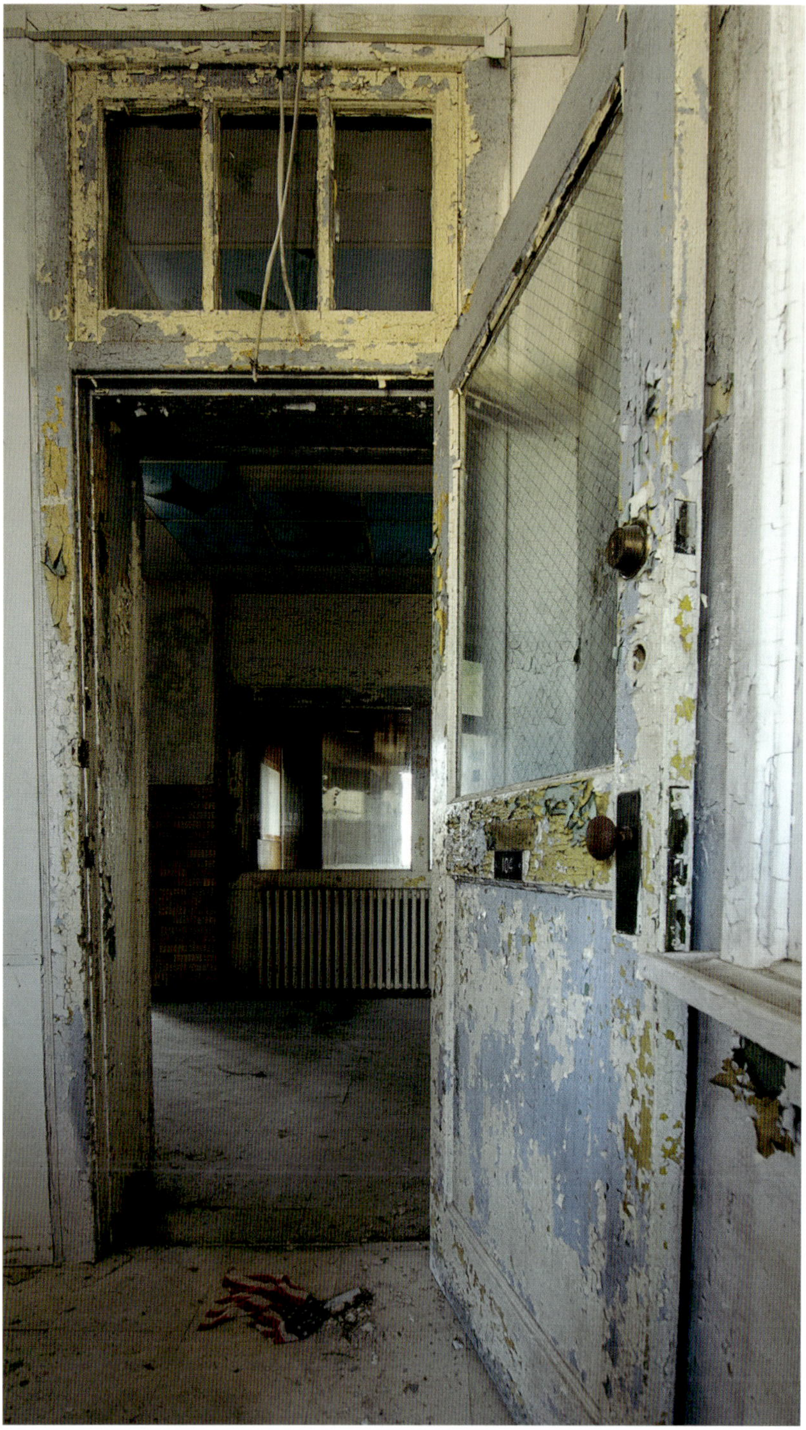

Lead paint peels off the walls.

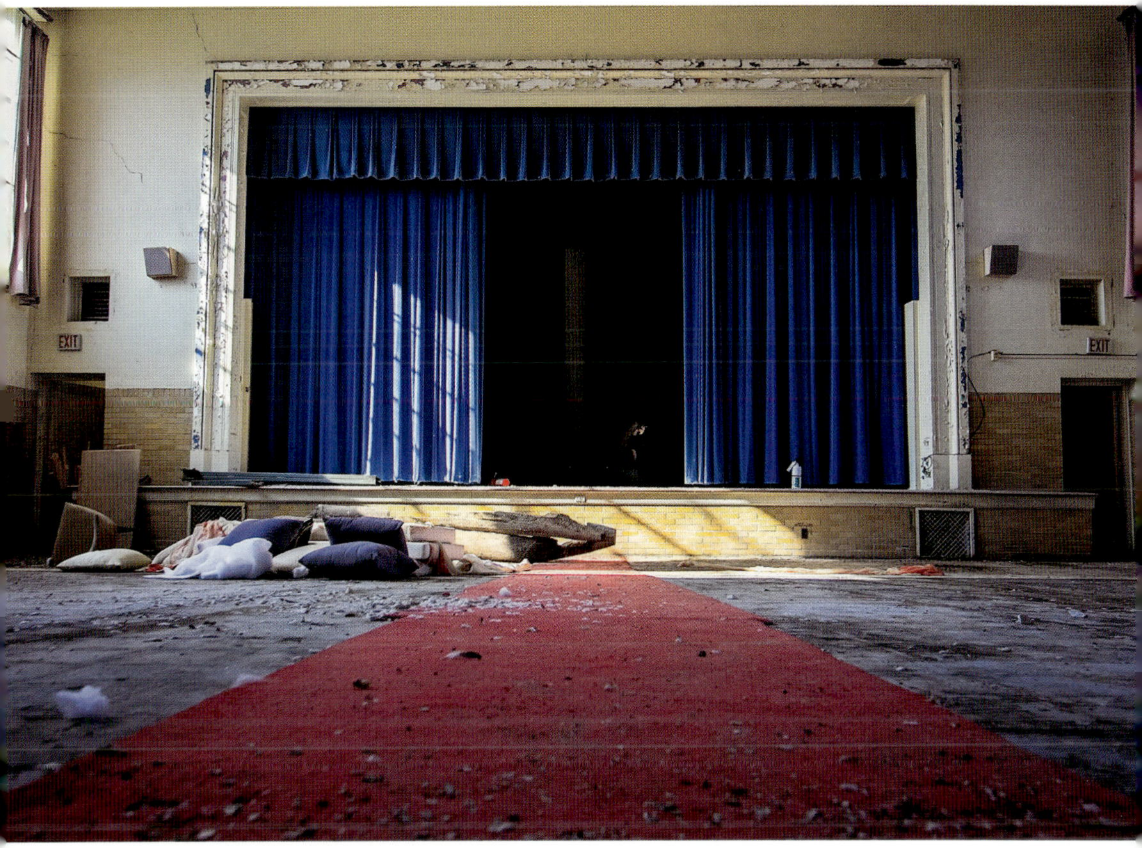

Red carpet down the main aisle in the auditorium.

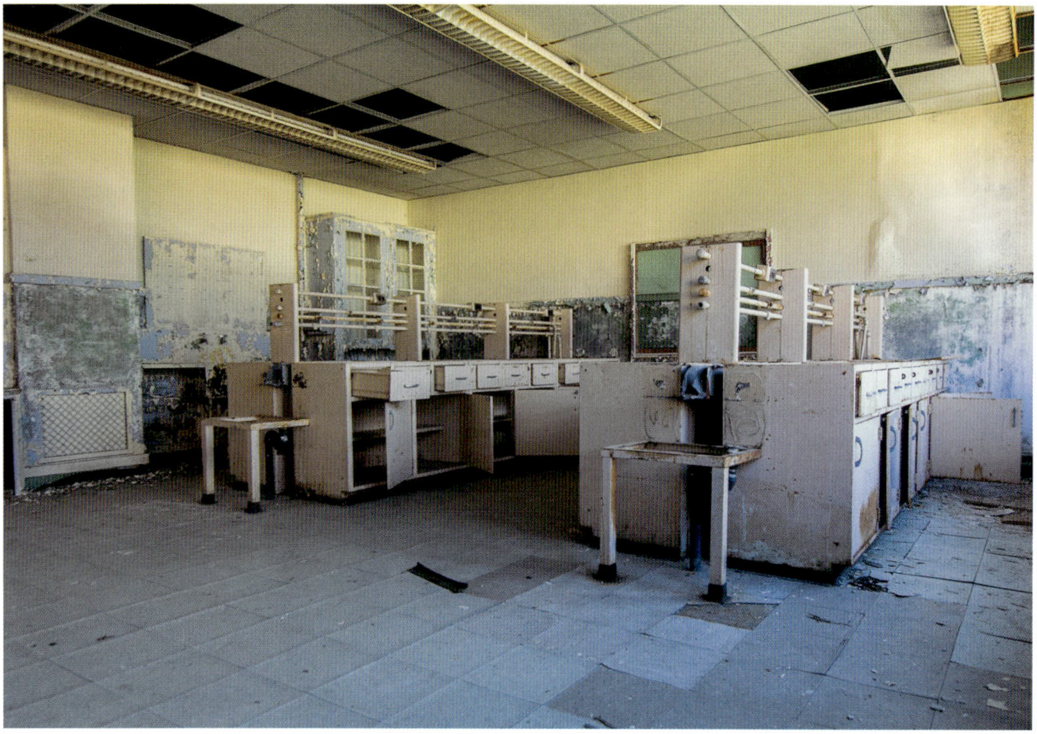

An empty science lab in an old school.

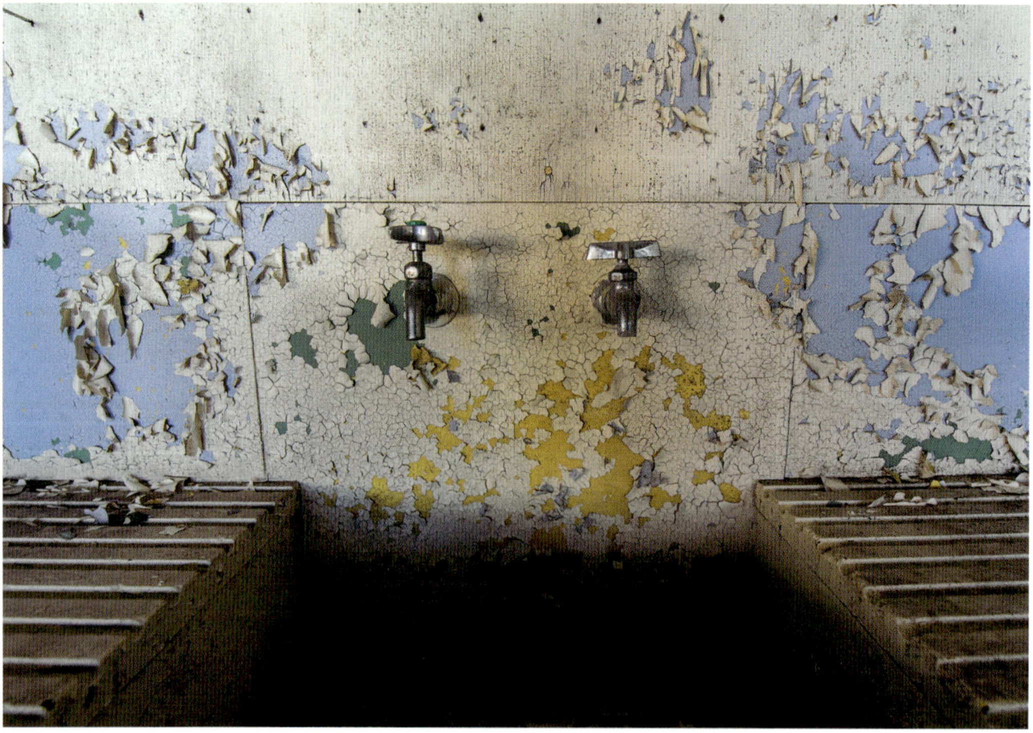

Faucets on the wall of the science lab.

Oak Grove Elementary School

History alone cannot always save a building from being abandoned. Outside of this school was a historical marker, telling visitors that George Washington attended school here for two years, from 1744-1746. The school was eventually demolished, and a Dollar General store now occupies the grounds. The historical marker is still standing.

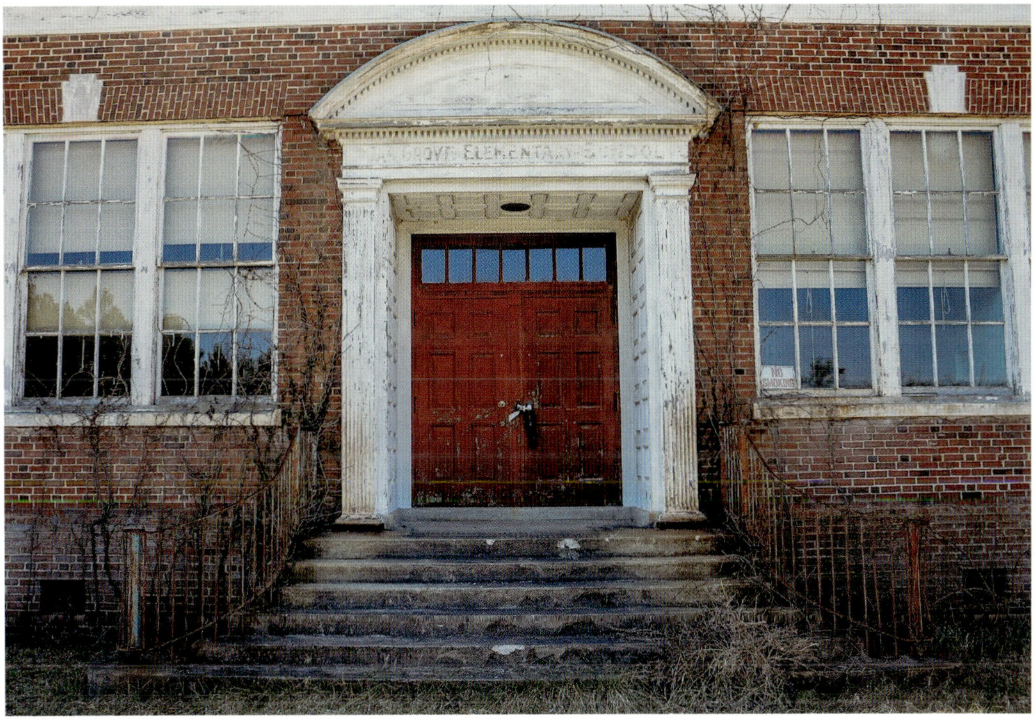

The entrance to the former Oak Grove Elementary school.

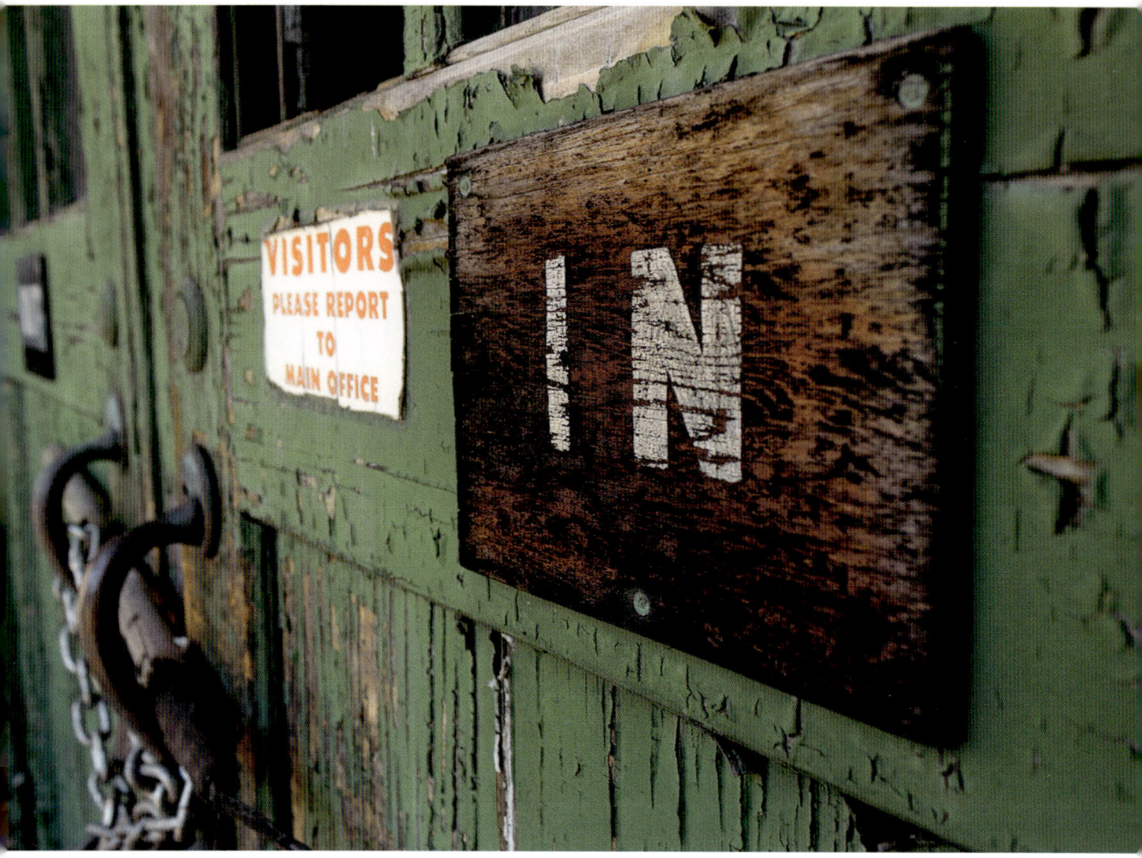

A sign welcomes visitors on the old green door.

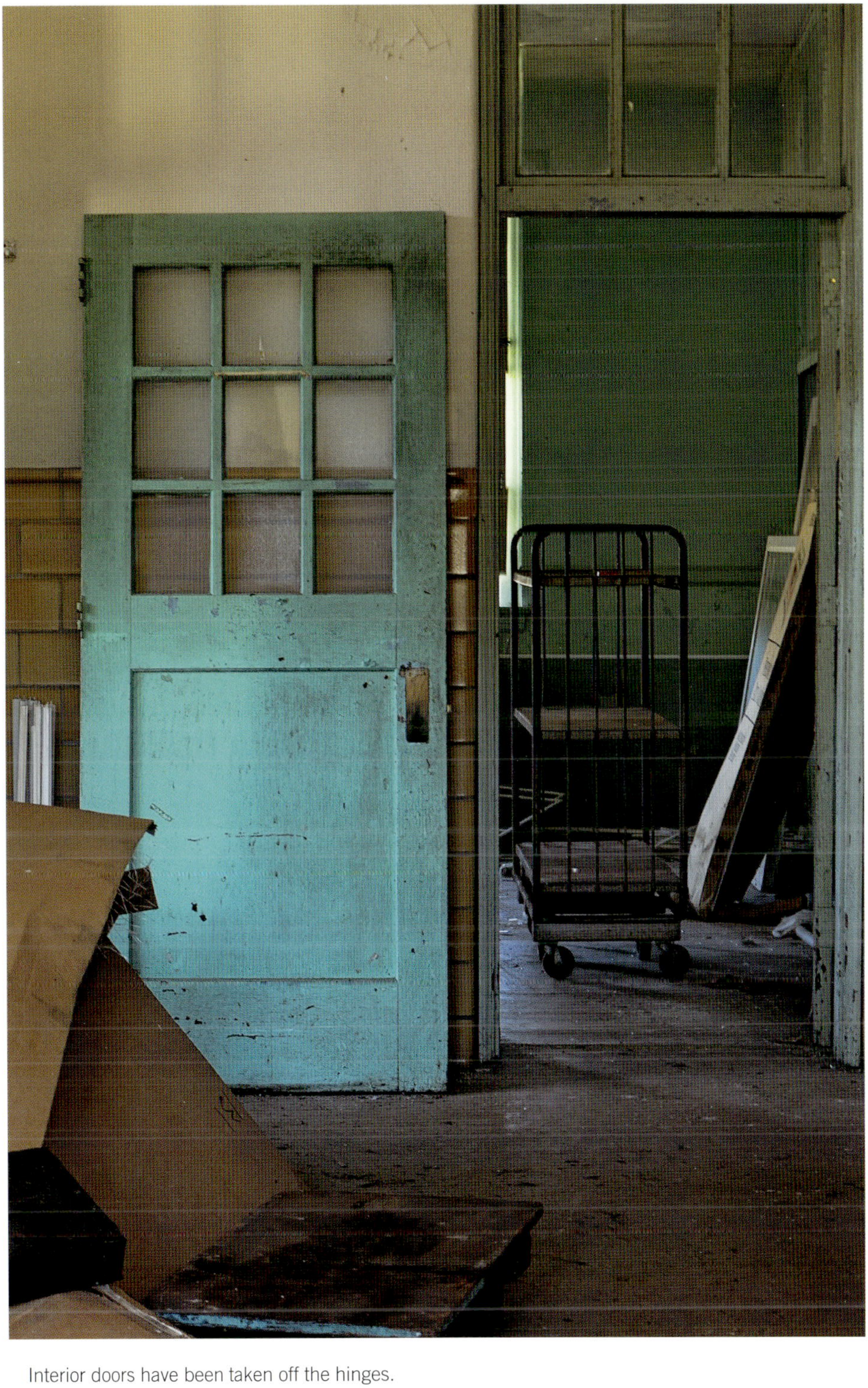

Interior doors have been taken off the hinges.

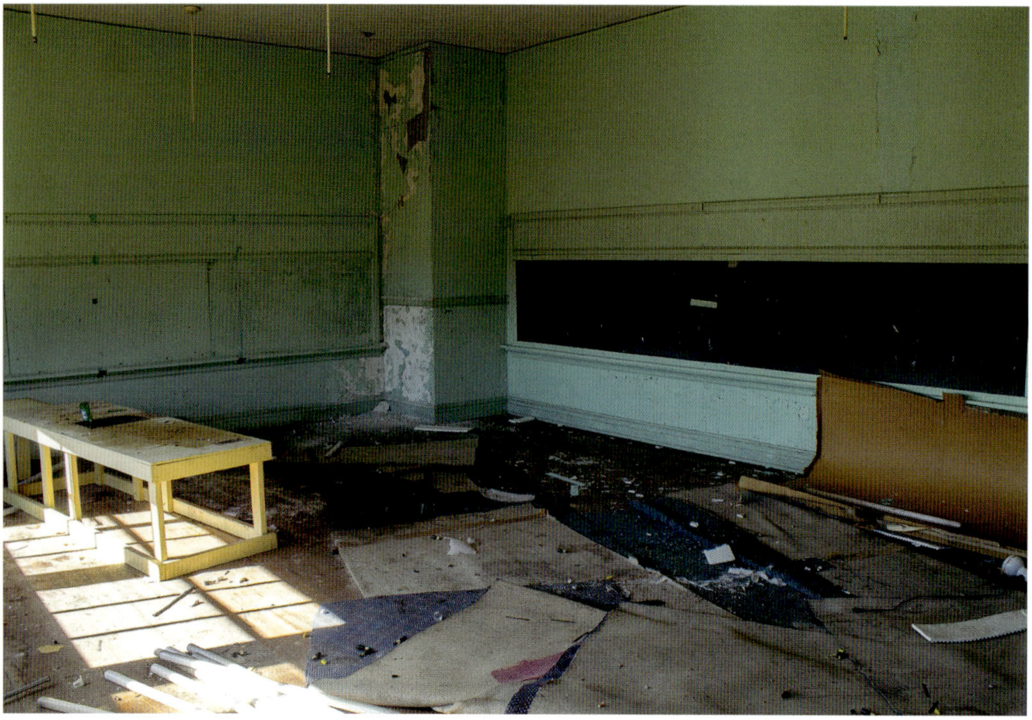

Empty classroom in Oak Grove Elementary.

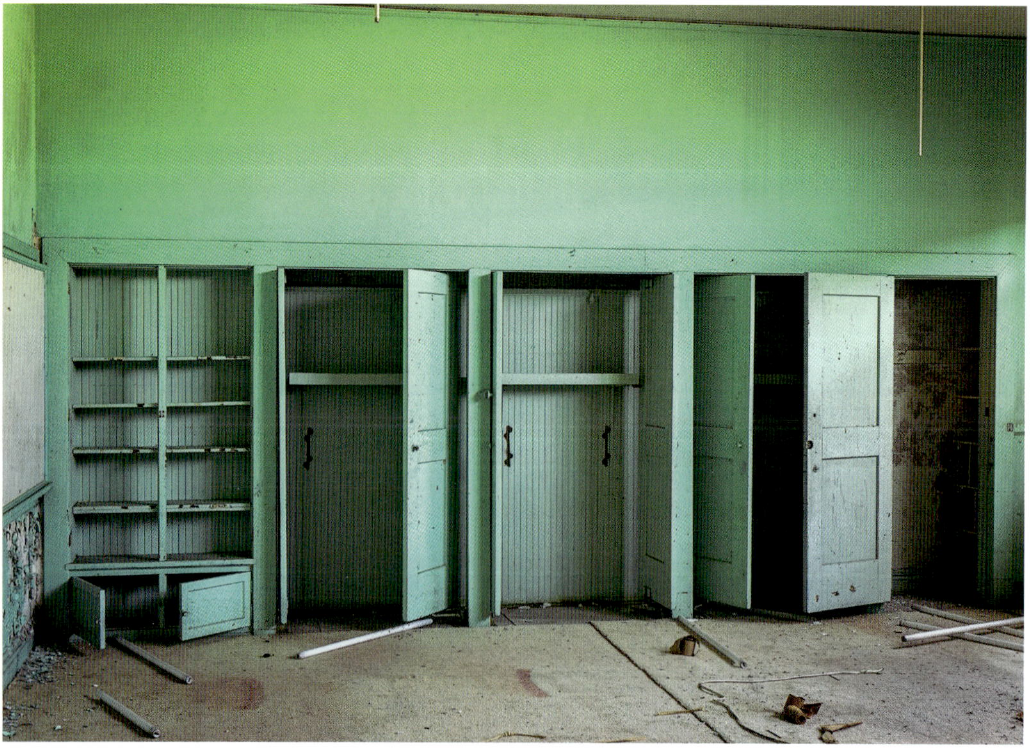

Coat closet in one of the classrooms.

TWIN SCHOOLS

The former elementary school was built in 1908, and the accompanying administration building in 1918. These buildings have been purchased by a private preservation society to save them from demolition, with a future goal of renovating them into upscale rental apartments.

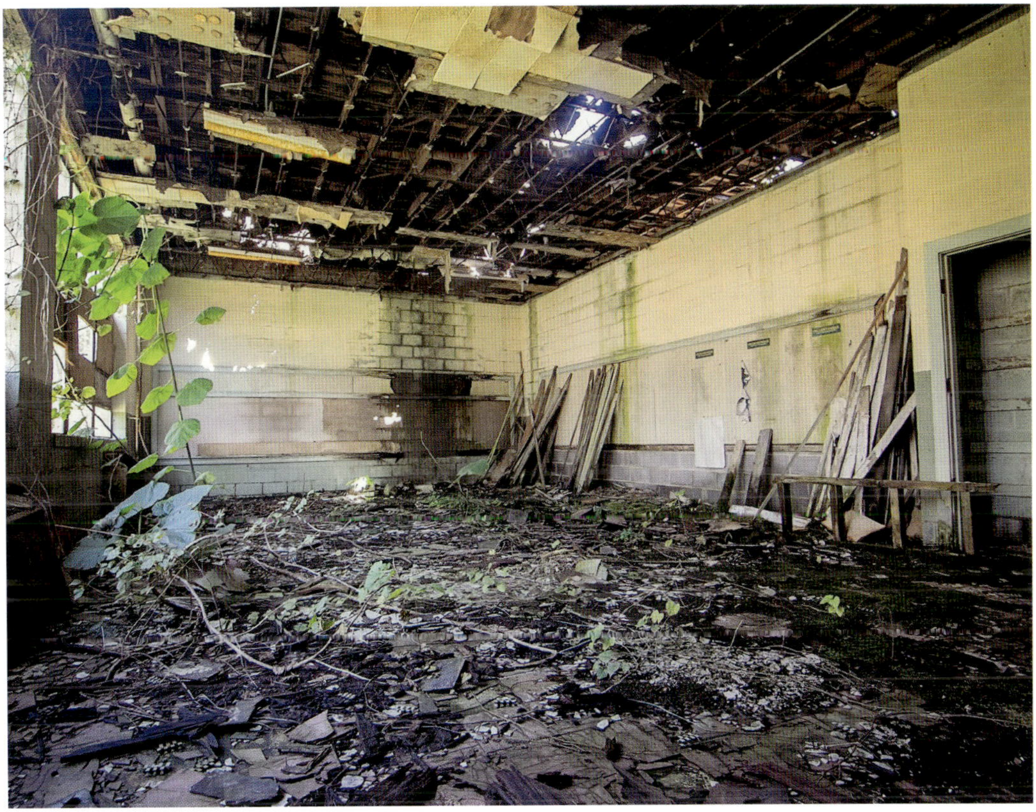

Nature takes over an old classroom.

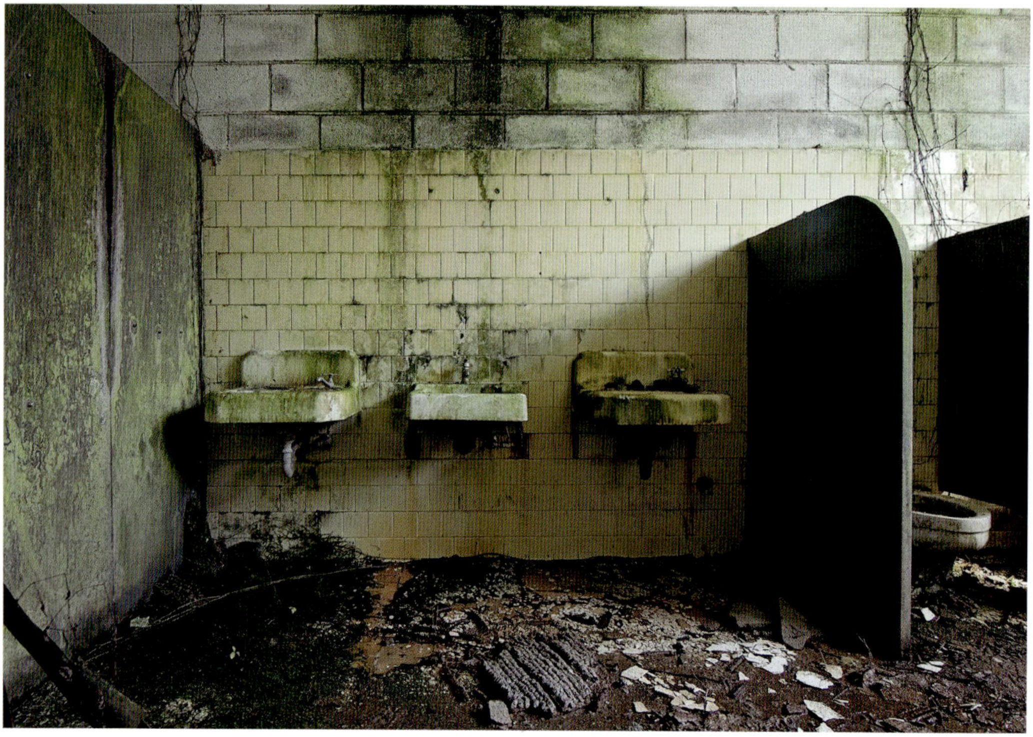

Moss and mold growing in the old bathroom.

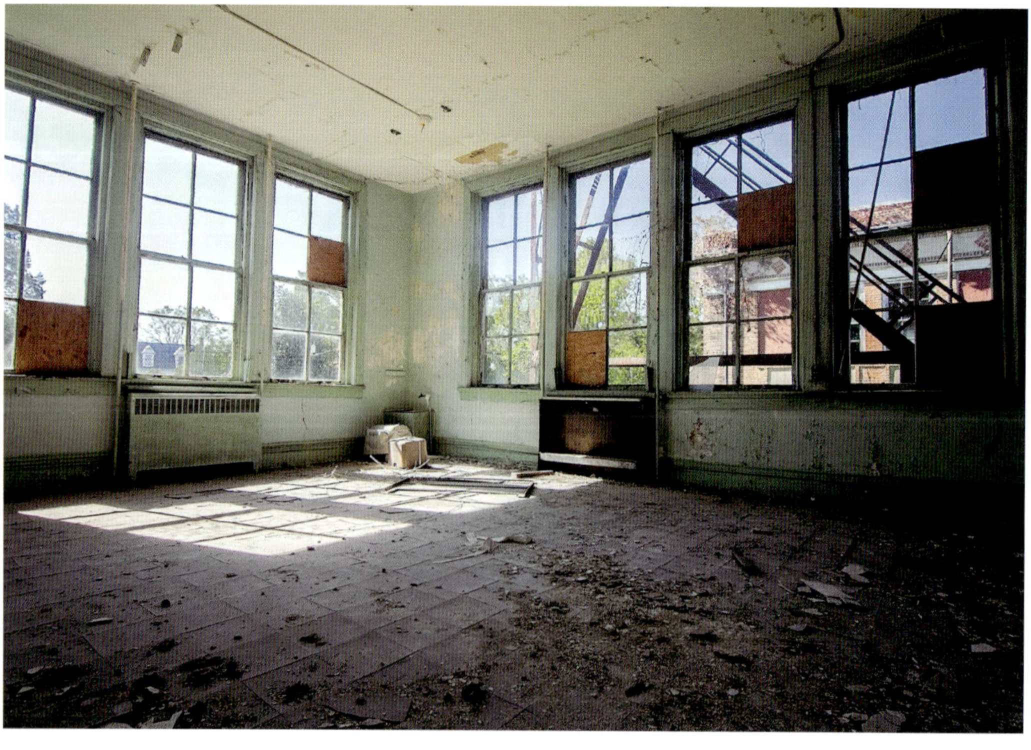

An upstairs classroom with lots of windows for natural light.

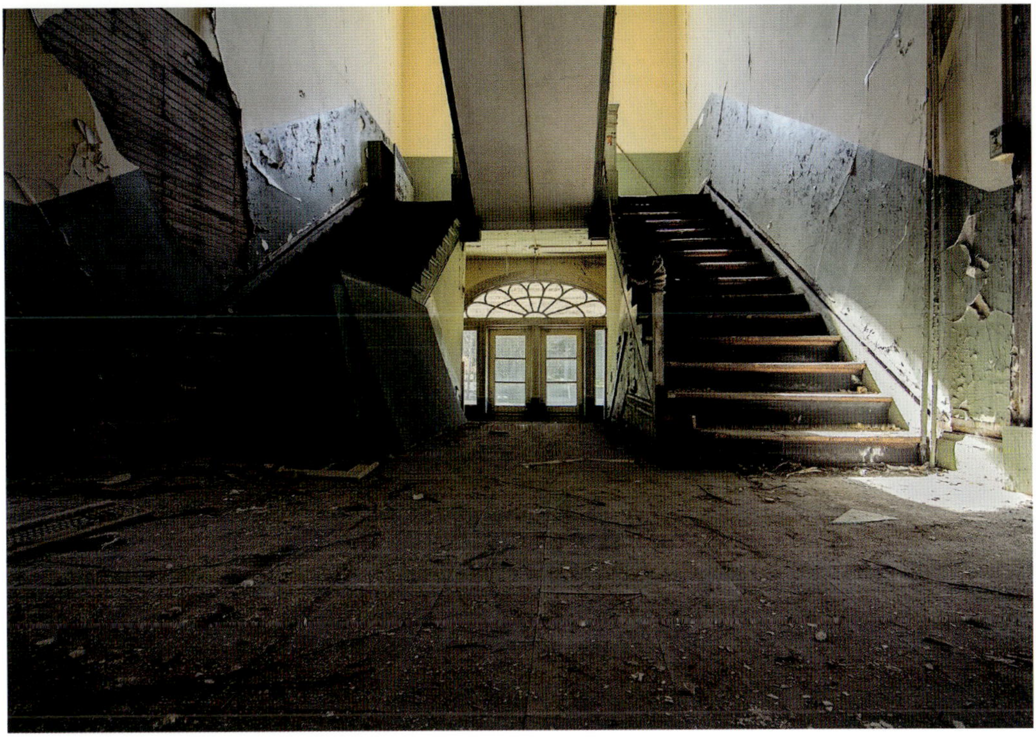

The stairway.

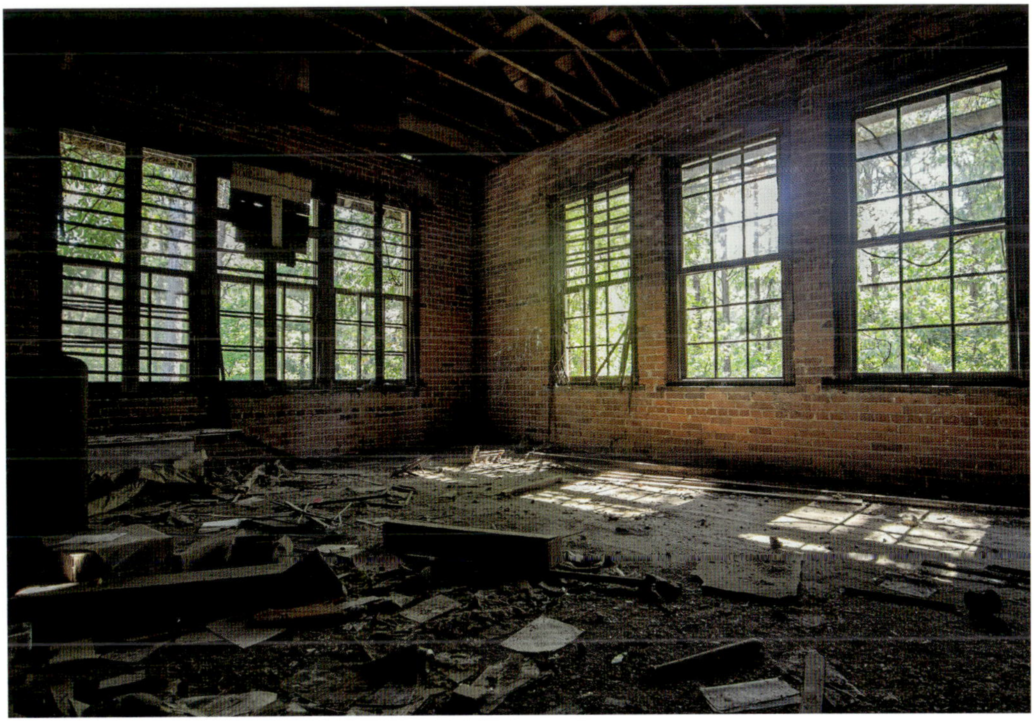

An empty classroom in an abandoned school.

PRINCE EDWARD SCHOOL

This former elementary school was built in 1915 for white children during segregation. It served as a school for grades 1-7 and had a capacity of 280 children. This is the older of the two original buildings, and the only one left standing.

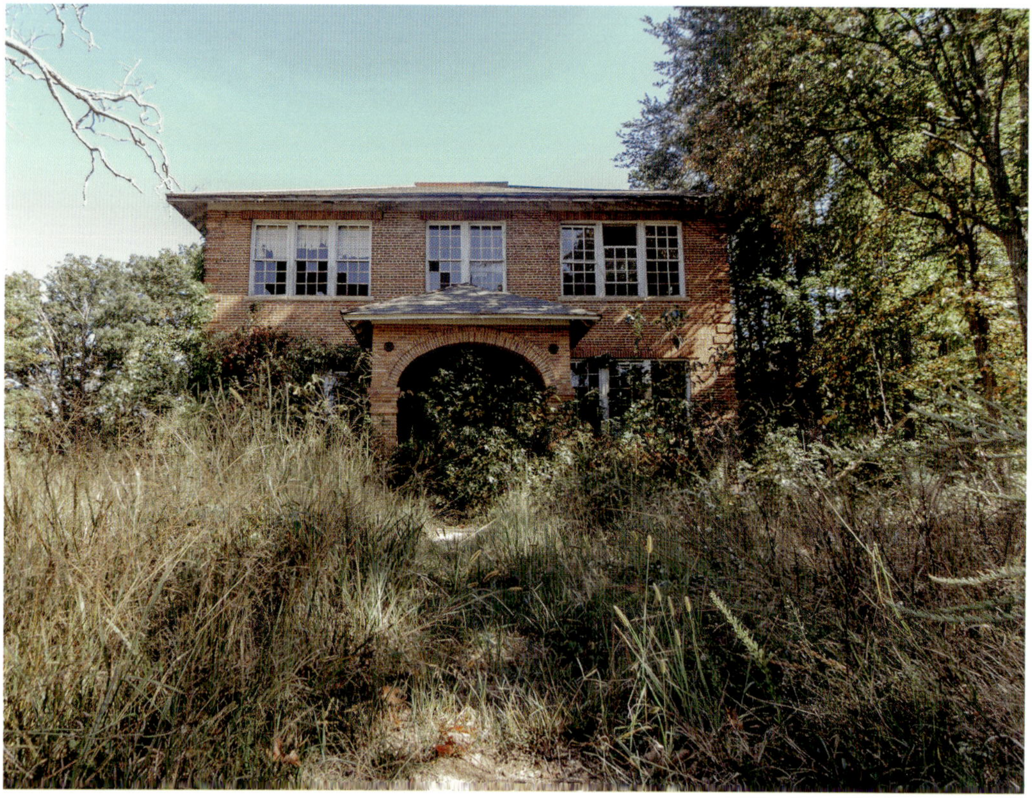

The overgrown front entrance of an old school. The school was infested with fleas.

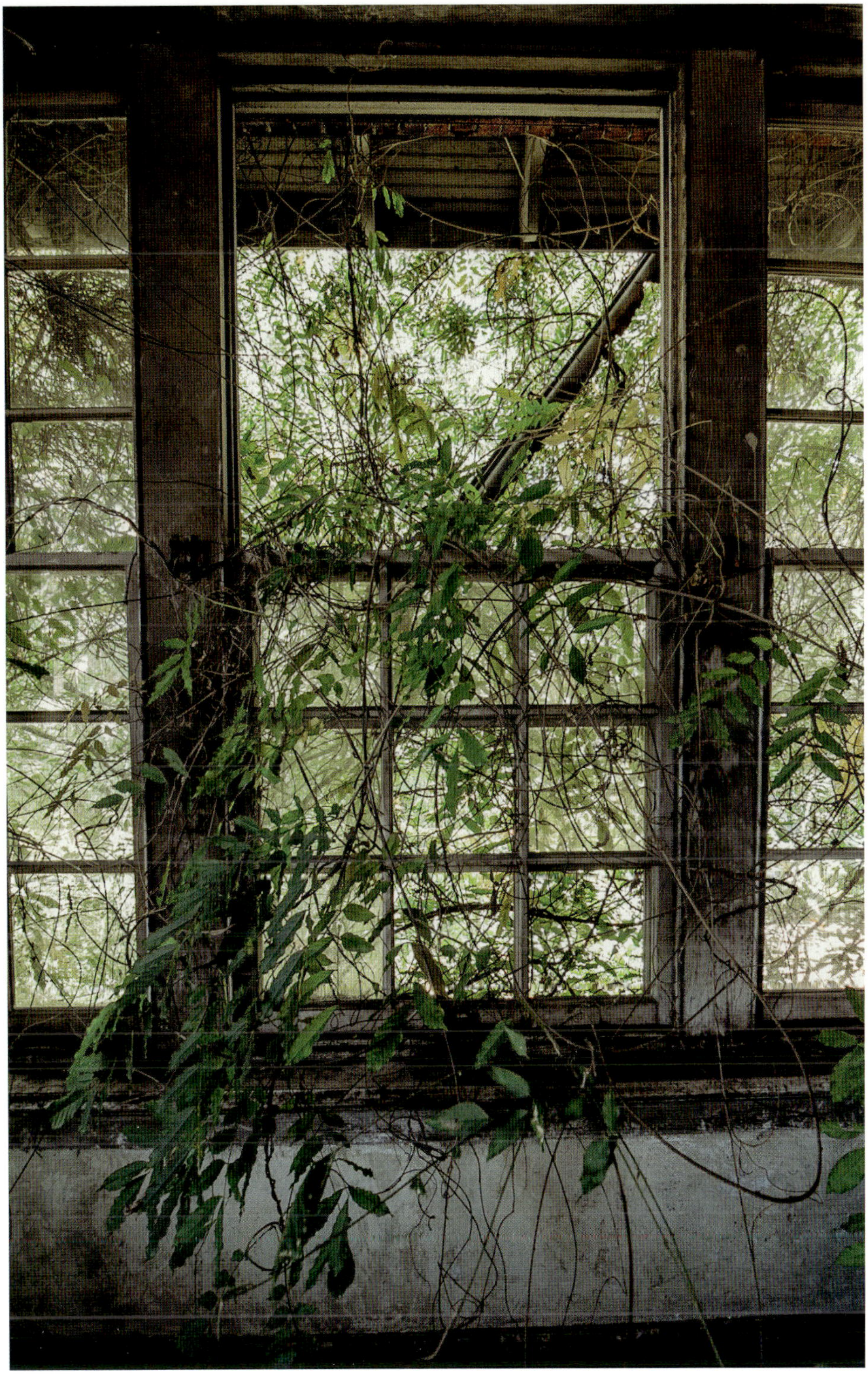

Plants grow through the windows in a classroom.

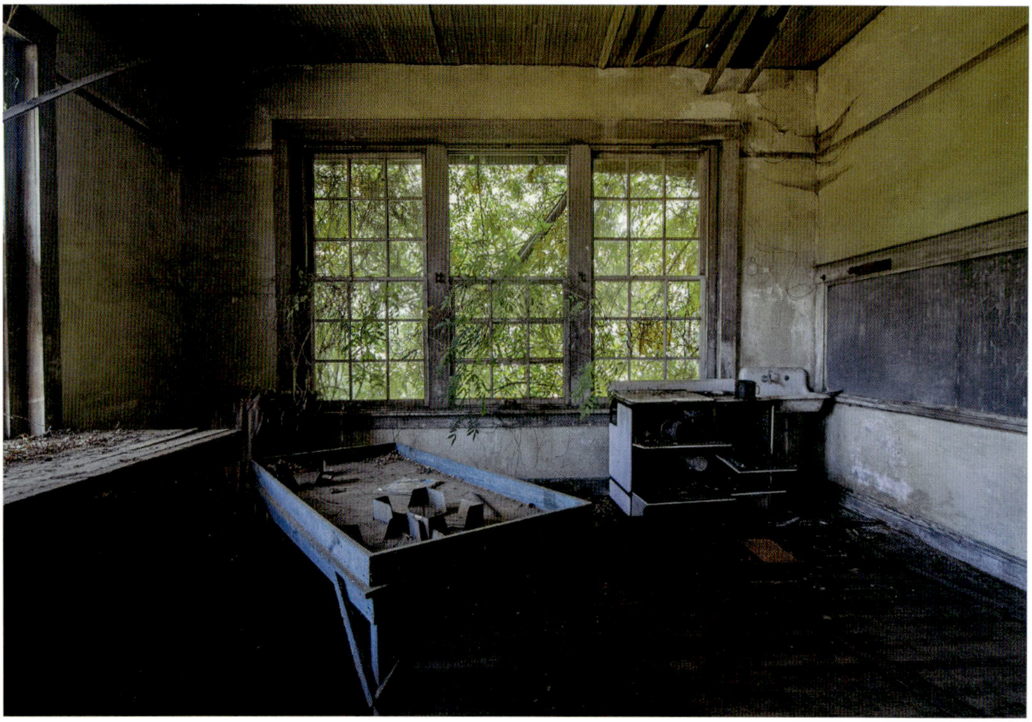

Remnants of the school kitchen mixed with a classroom.

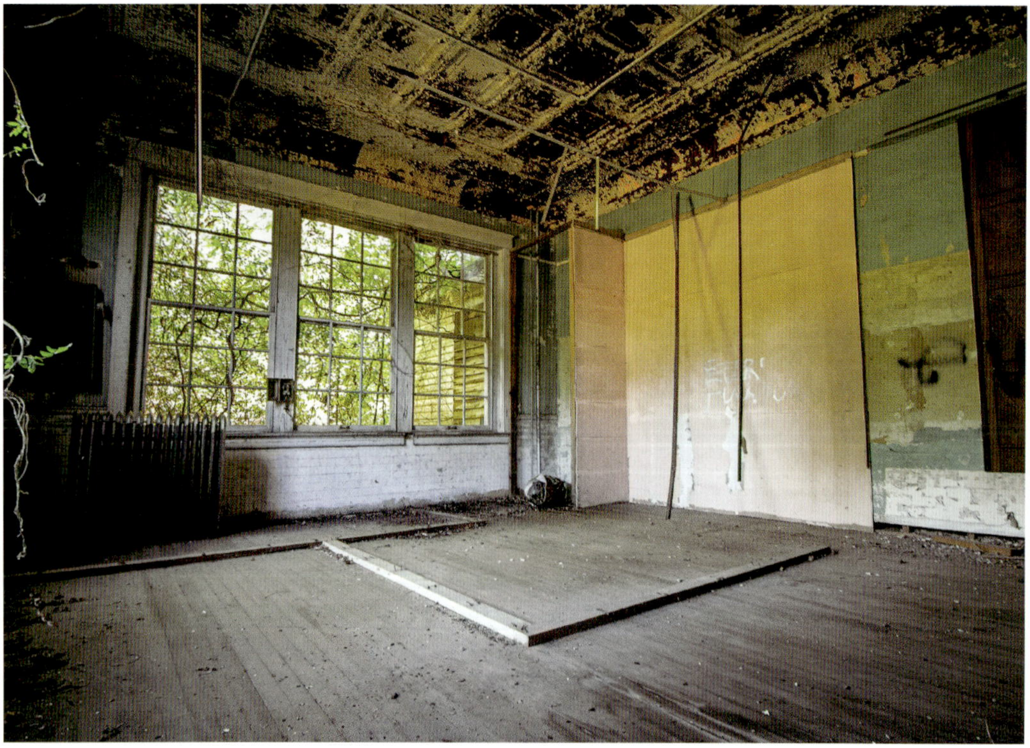

Another empty classroom.

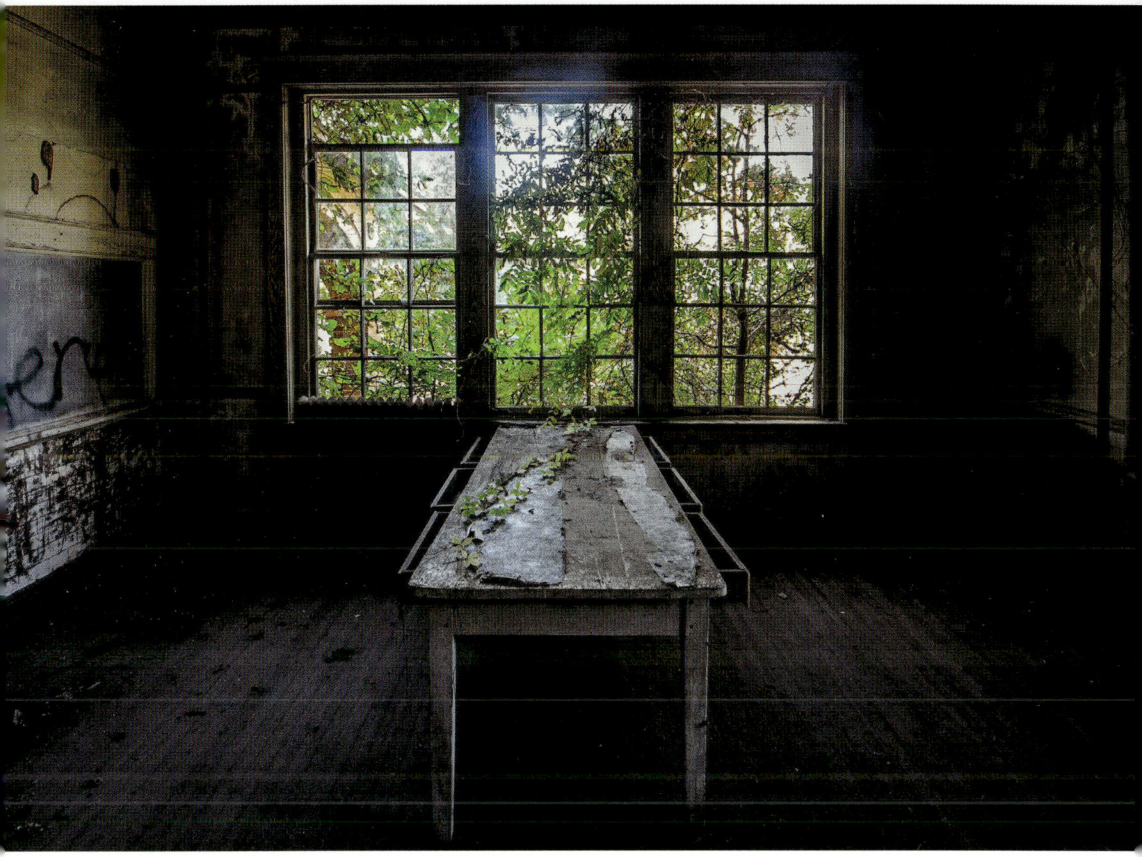

Just a single table is left behind.

Countryside Schools

These photos are a collection of abandoned schools scattered across the Virginia countryside. At one time, they were all centerpieces of their communities. The names and history of several of these schools have been purposely left out to keep their identity safe. Unfortunately, with many schools, most of the records were not kept, or transferred digitally, so little history is known about some of the other small community schools.

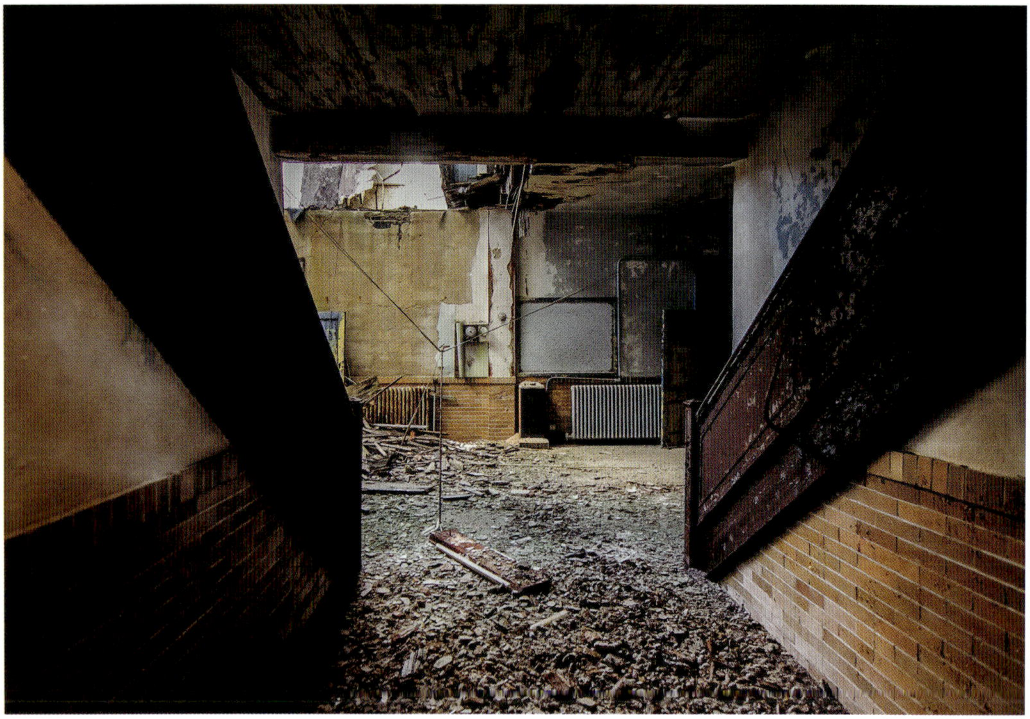

What's left of the main school entrance.

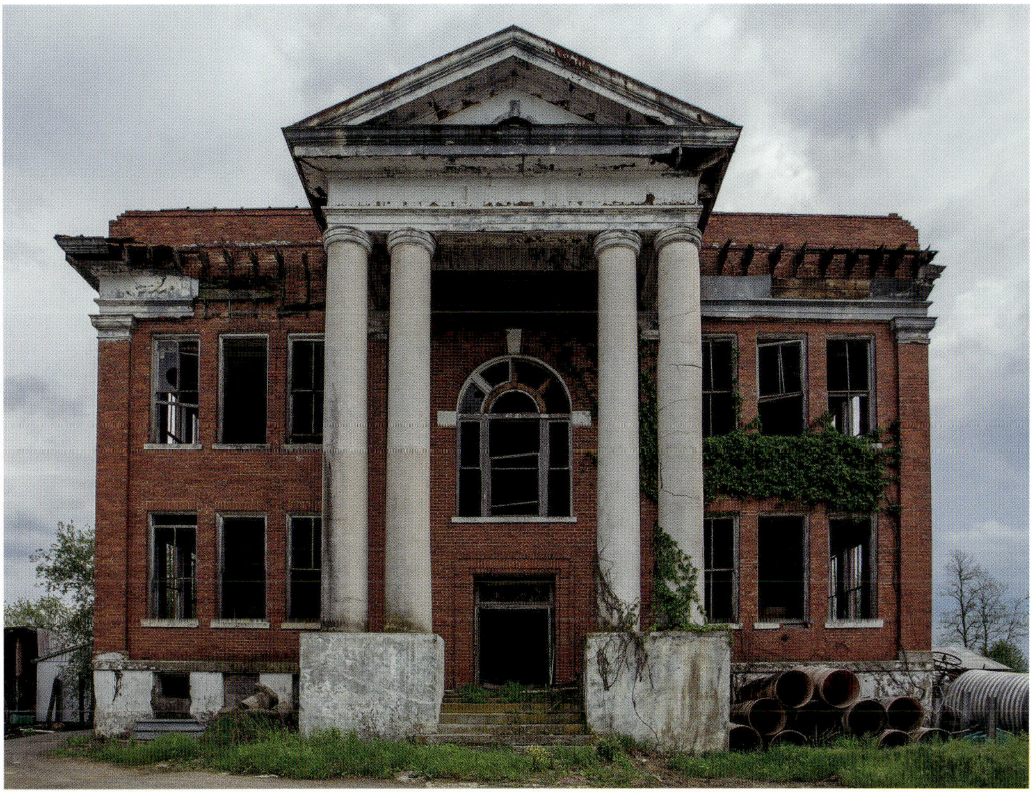

The grand entrance and columns of an old country school.

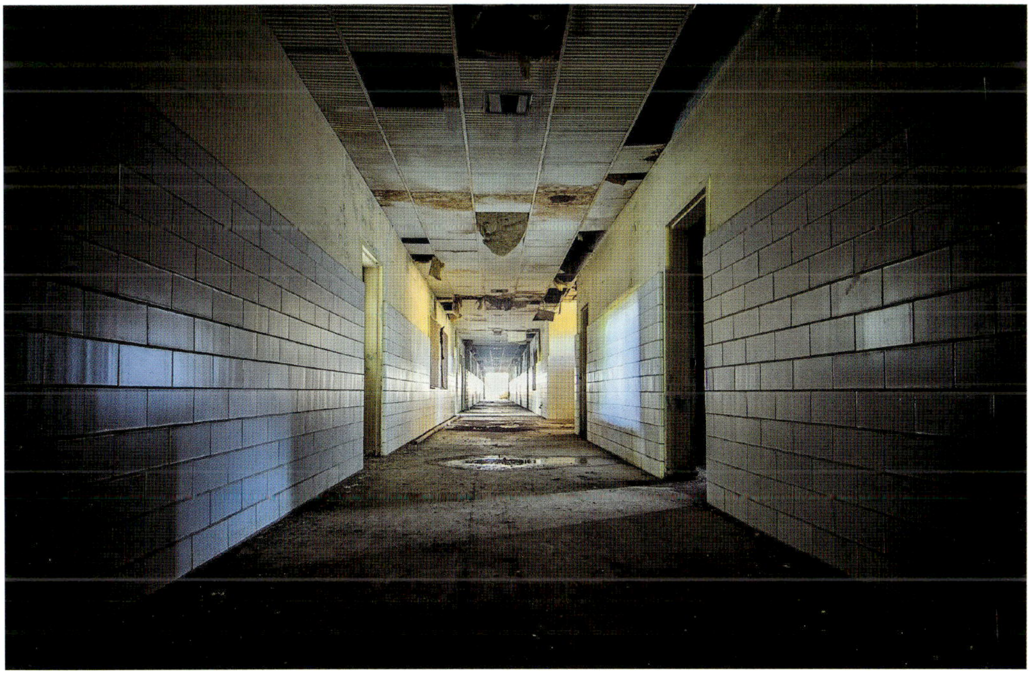

Shadows lead the way in the empty hallways.

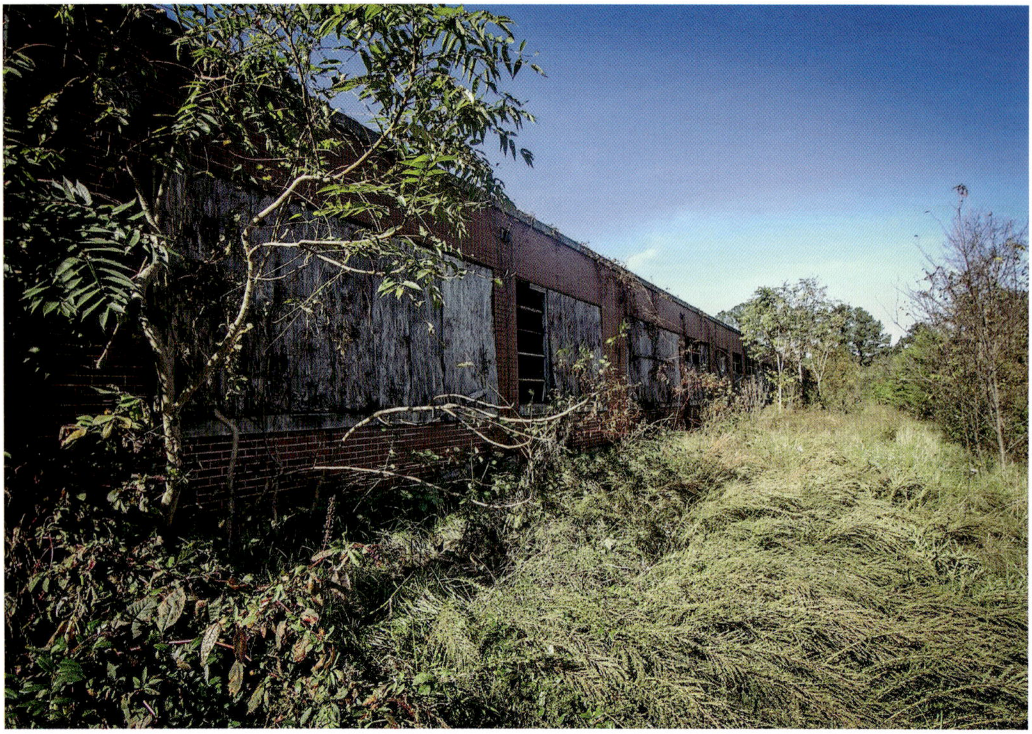

This school is slowly being reclaimed by nature.

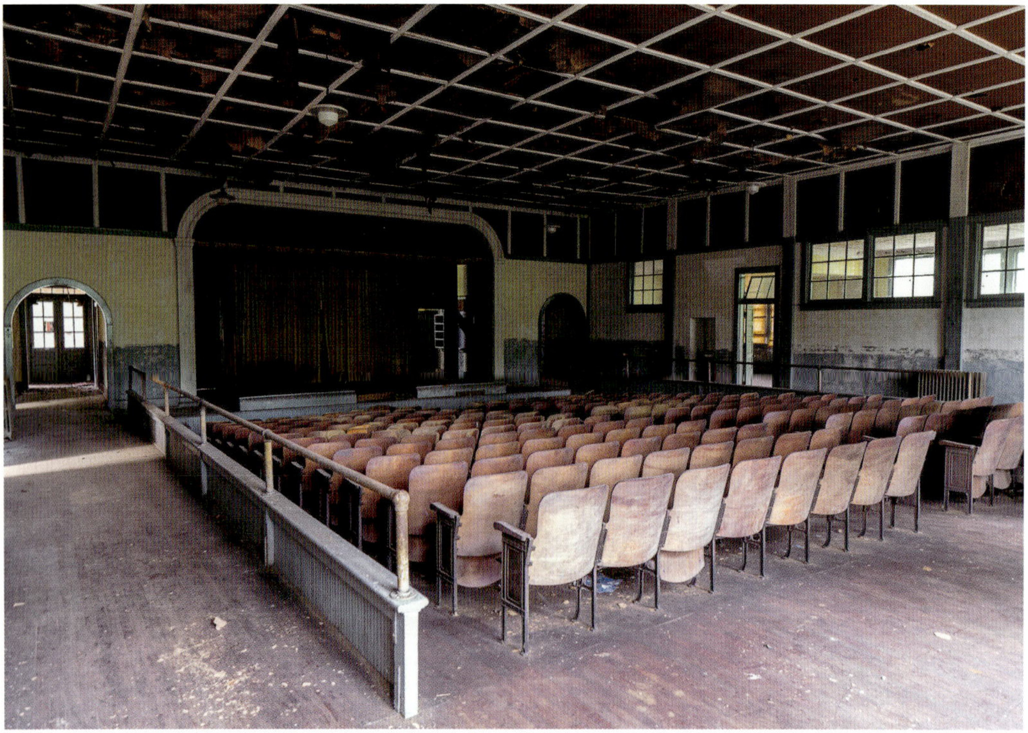

The auditorium is still fully intact with chairs and the stage curtain.

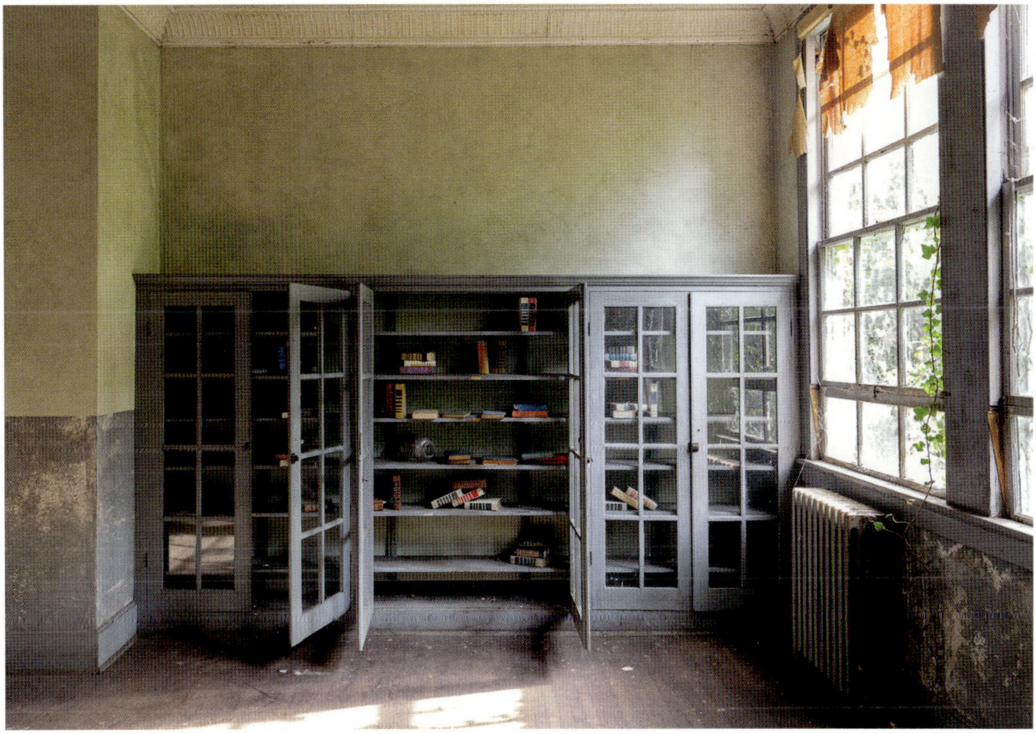

The book case of a classroom with books still on the shelves.

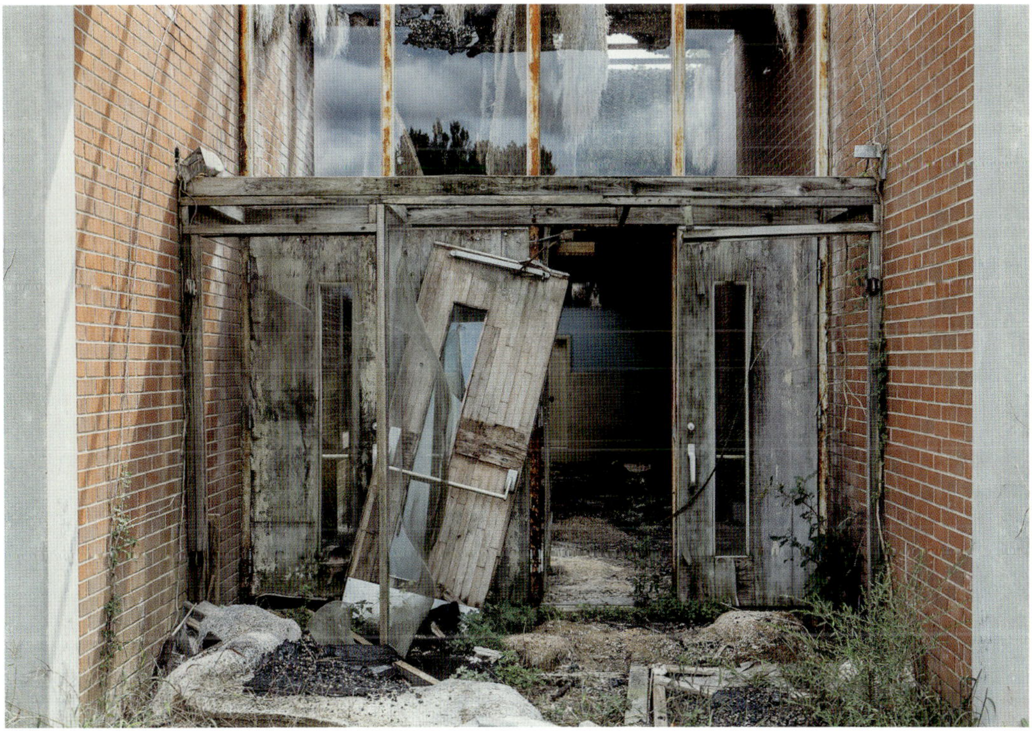

The school's main doors are broken off, and barely hanging on.

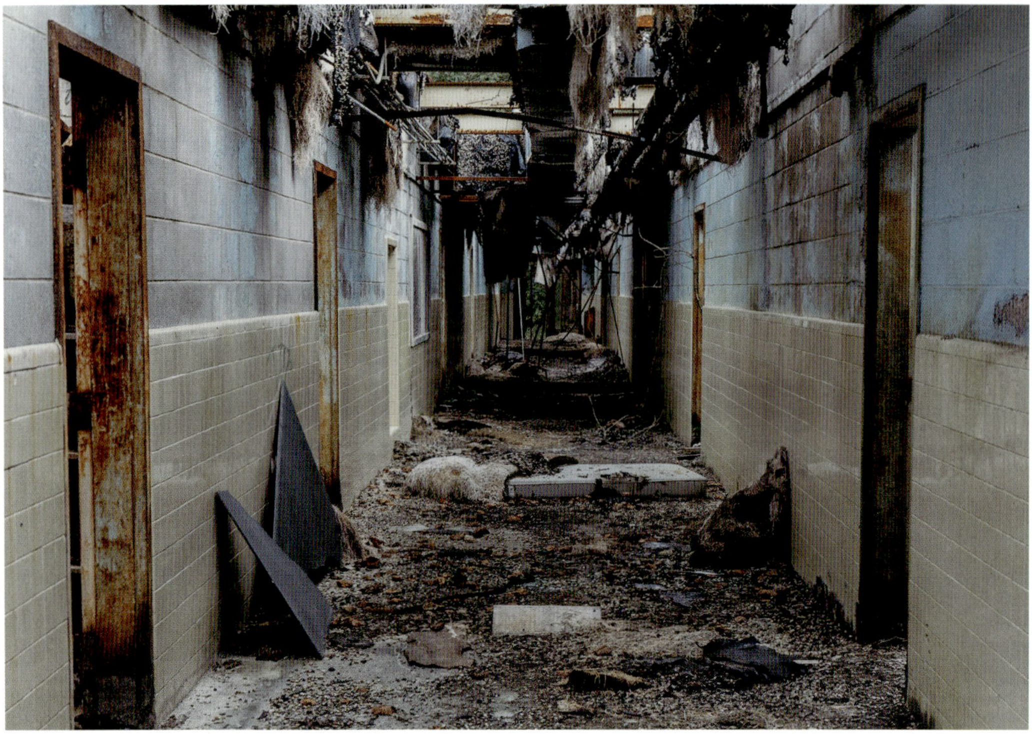

Traditional tile hallways in an old elementary school.

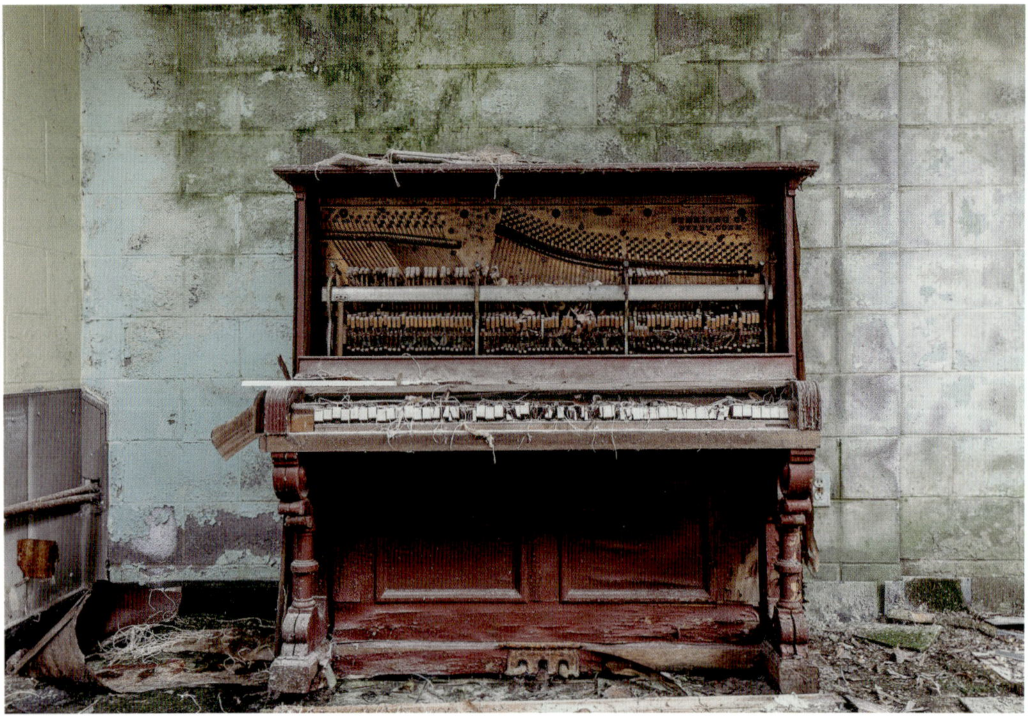

A piano left behind in the multipurpose cafeteria/gym room.

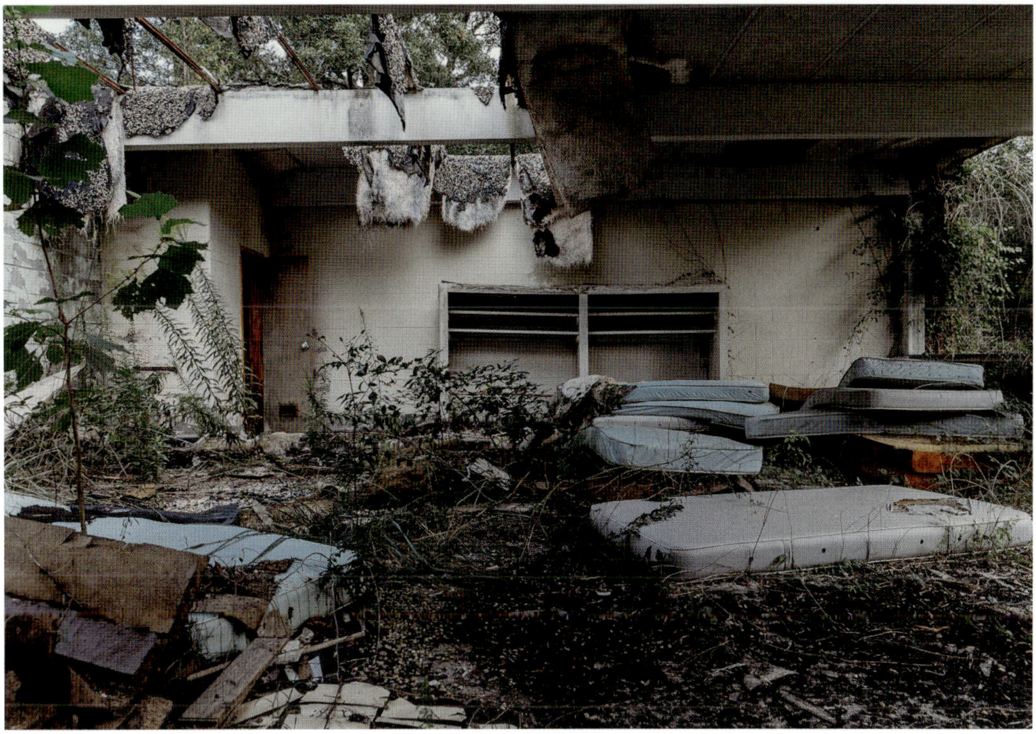

Old mattresses remain from when the school was used as a home for the elderly.

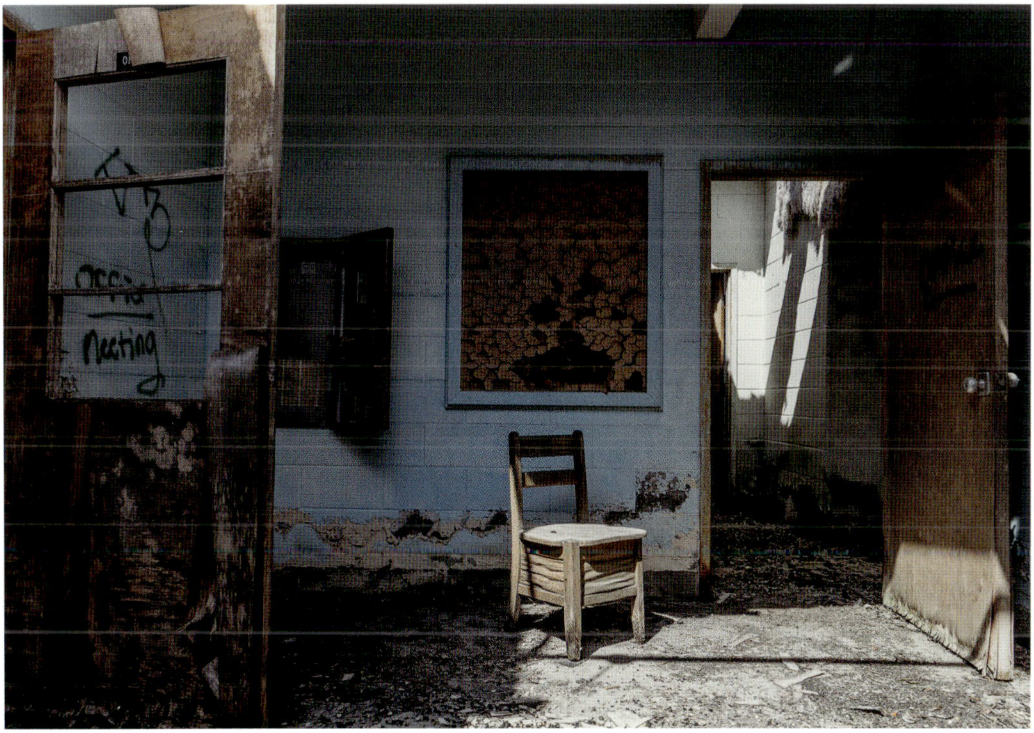

The waiting room when students were sent to see the principal.

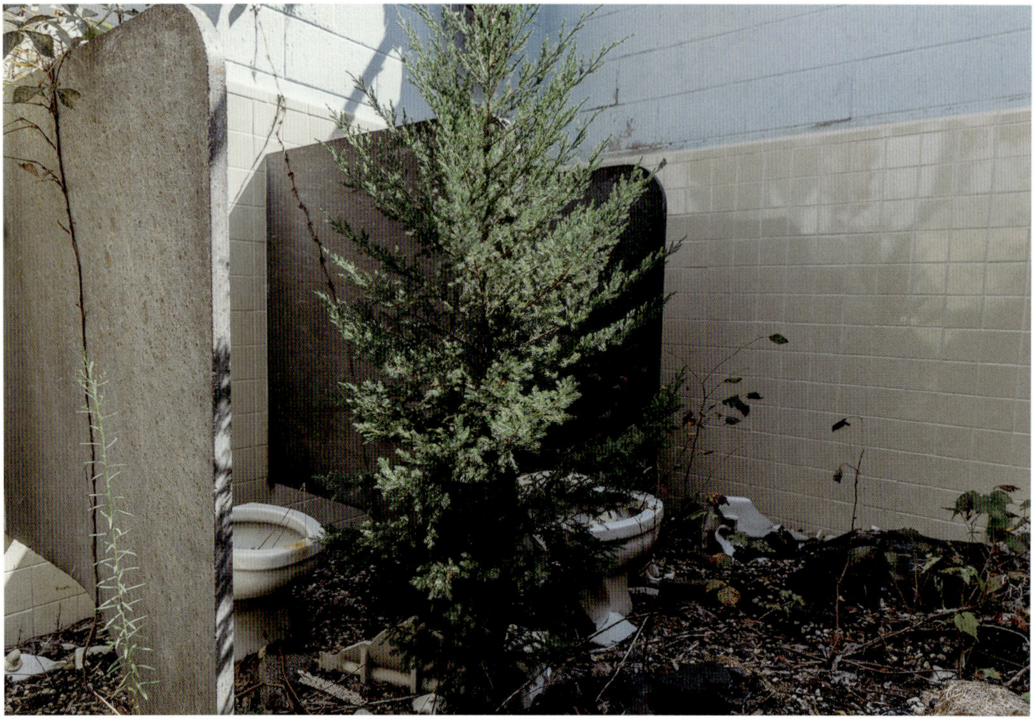

The remains of one of the buildings after the fire.

4

ABANDONED MILL

For many years, Richmond has been a center of economic activity. The growth of industry in the city can be traced back to the Reconstruction Era after the Civil War. These industries included more traditional interests, specifically railroads and tobacco processing.

The James River served as a primary transportation hub, bringing tobacco to Atlantic ports for shipment to Europe, eventually becoming an industrial waterway. Due to the increased and heavy traffic, by the mid-twentieth century, public access to the James River was prohibited due to its high level of pollution.

Over the decades, these industries around Richmond have died off, and mostly given way to a heavier focus in the legal, financial, and governmental sectors.

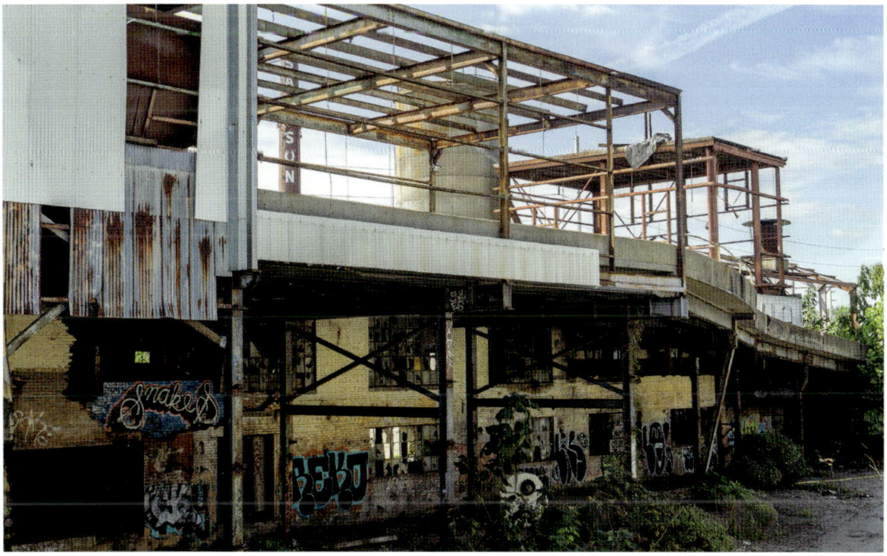

What remains of the mill's exterior.

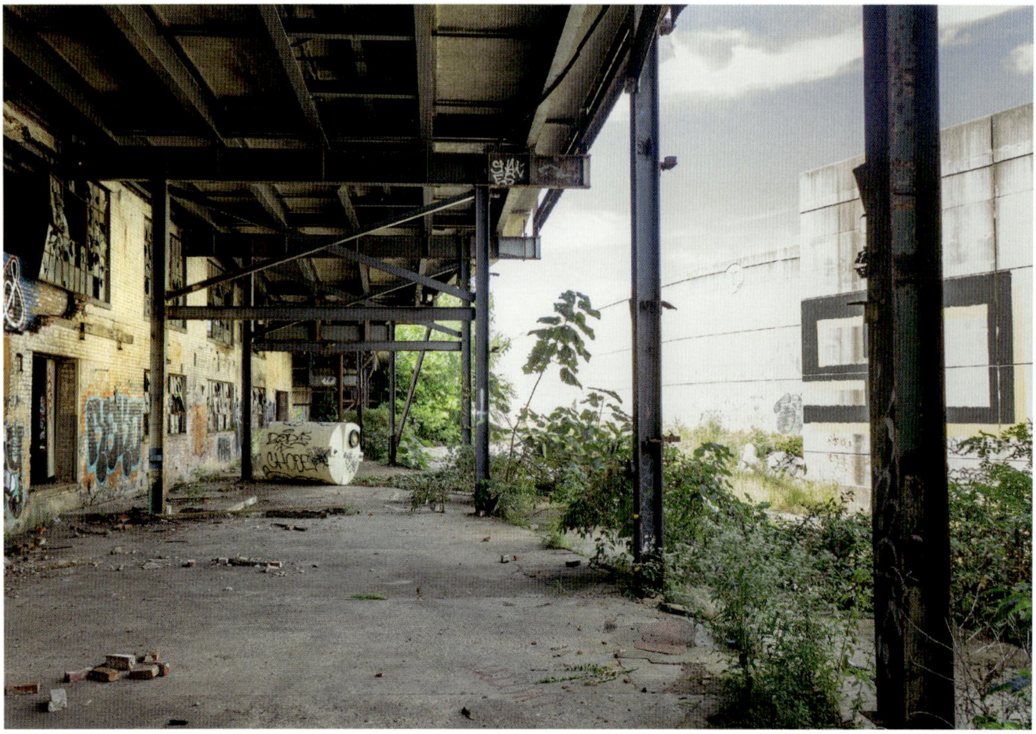

Another view from outside of the abandoned mill.

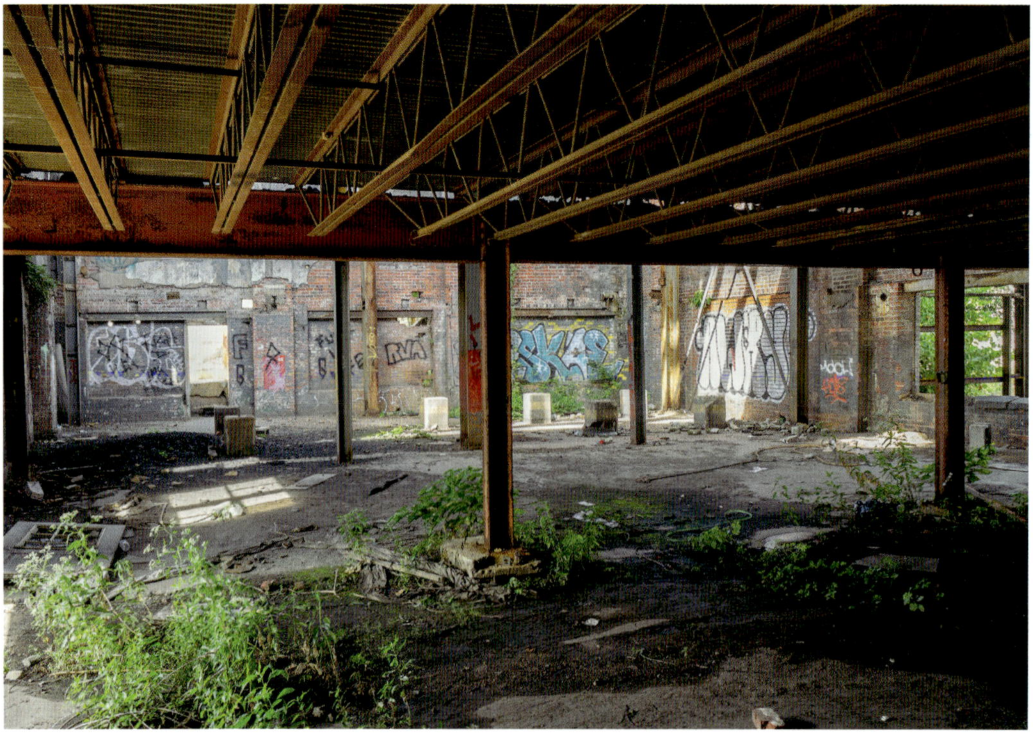

Plants begin to grow inside the abandoned mill.

Various Mills

As previously mentioned, mills of different kinds dot the landscape of Virginia. These industrial plants centered around paper, flour (gristmills), and textiles among others. Richmond's flour mills were heavily ingrained in trade with South Africa, and the iron mills helped supply a major demand for railroad iron across the nation. Here are a few examples of abandoned mills throughout Virginia, including some that have no documented history.

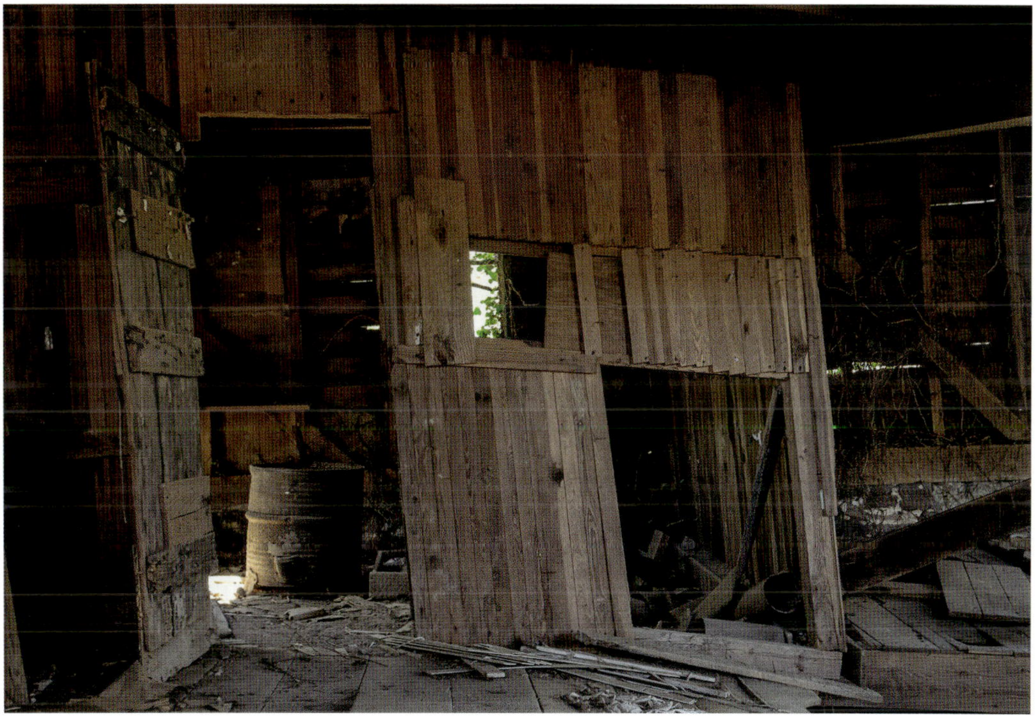

The old mill starts to shift and slowly falls down due to years of neglect.

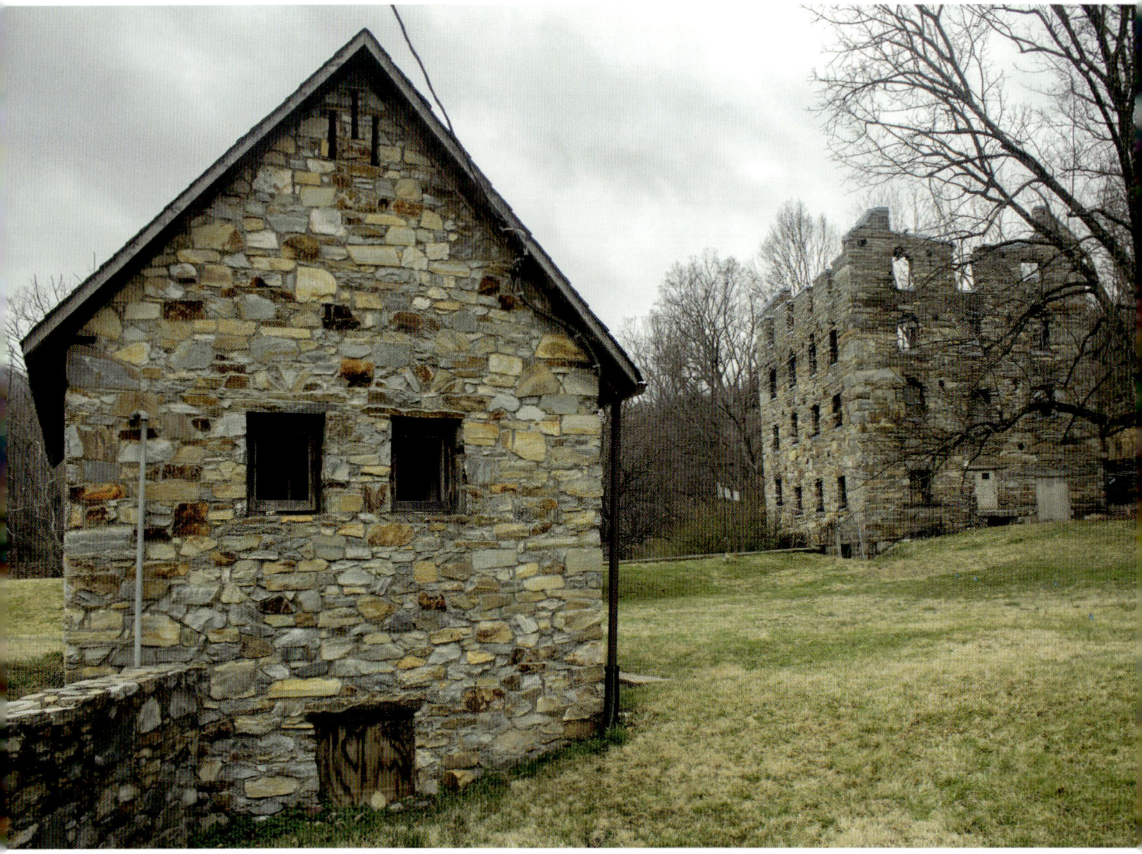

Beverley Mill, also known as Chapman Mill, was a historical grist mill that supplied food for five different wars.

Opposite page: The wooden exterior slowly deteriorates, and planks pull away from the structure.

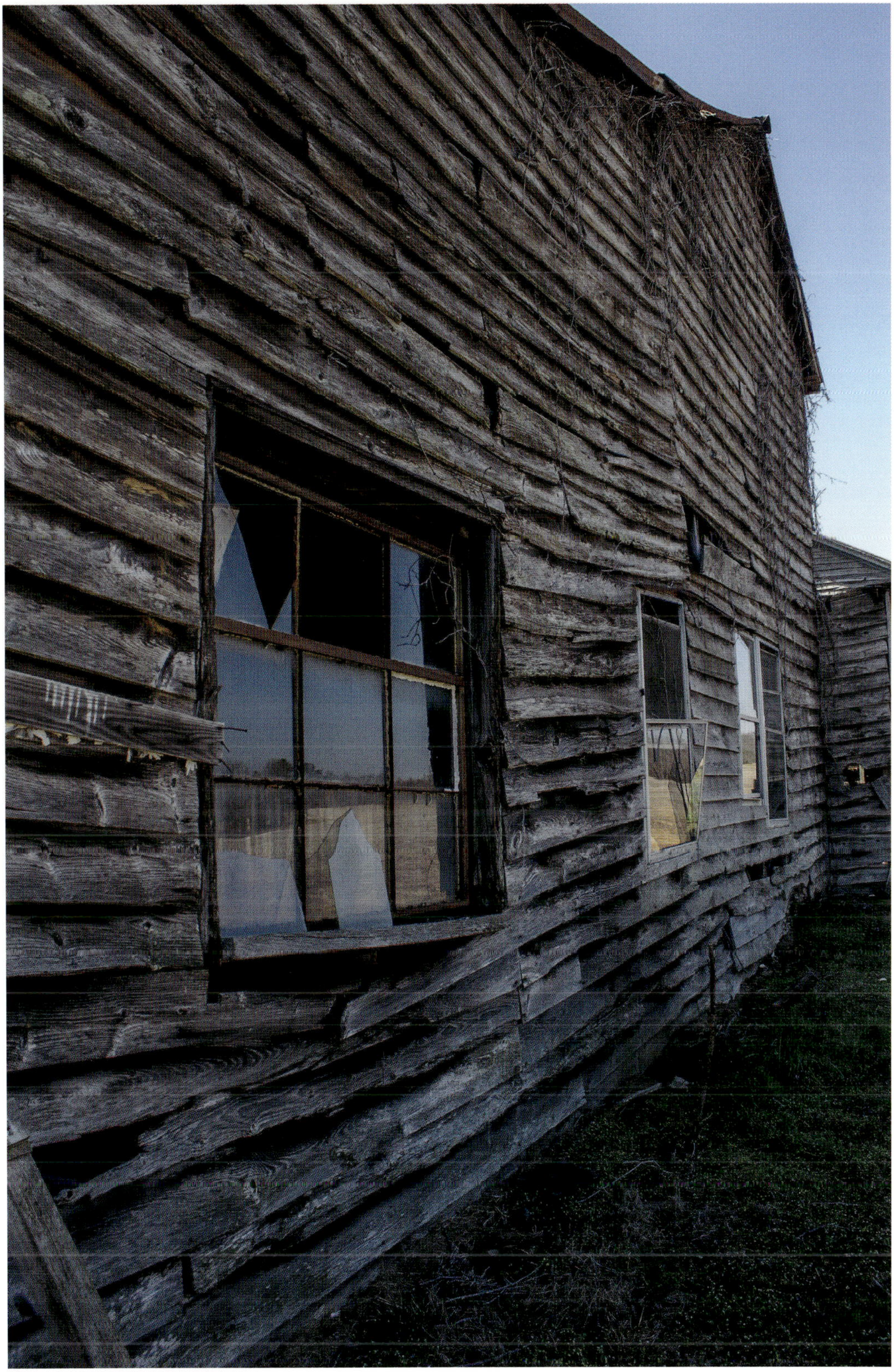

5

FULTON GAS WORKS

ILLUMINATING THE CITY OF RICHMOND

One of the most popular and well-known abandoned locations is the former Fulton Gas Works site in Richmond. For more than a century, Fulton Gas Works used to produce coal gas that was in turn used to power homes, businesses, and the streetlights in Richmond. This is not the type of natural gas that we commonly know of today that comes out of the ground. The gas was made by converting coal into a gas. One of the major side effects was leaving behind a toxic "tar" that is believed to contain 500 to 3,000 different mixtures that can be harmful to humans, animals, and plants.

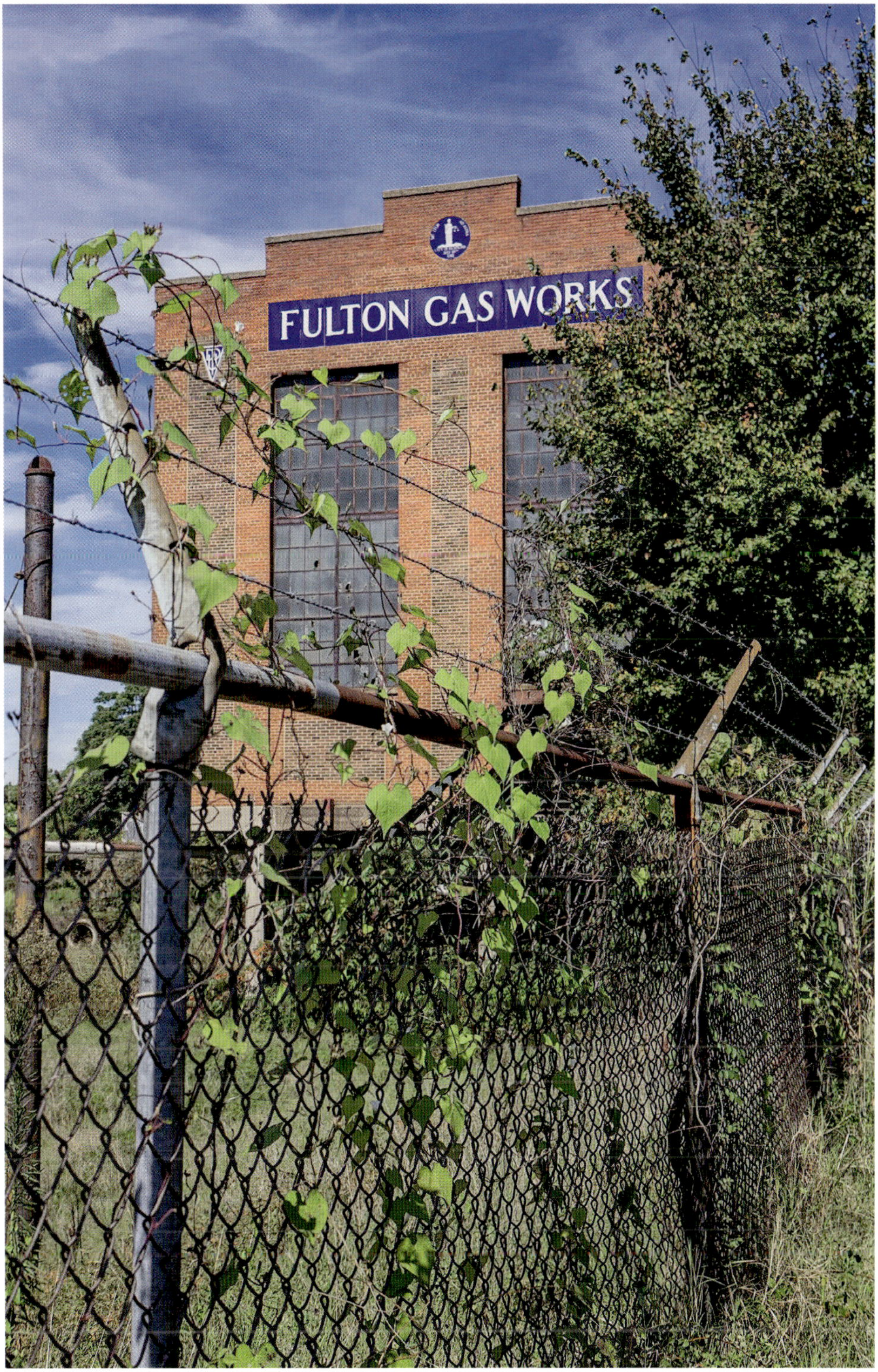

The signage on the Fulton Gas Works main building.

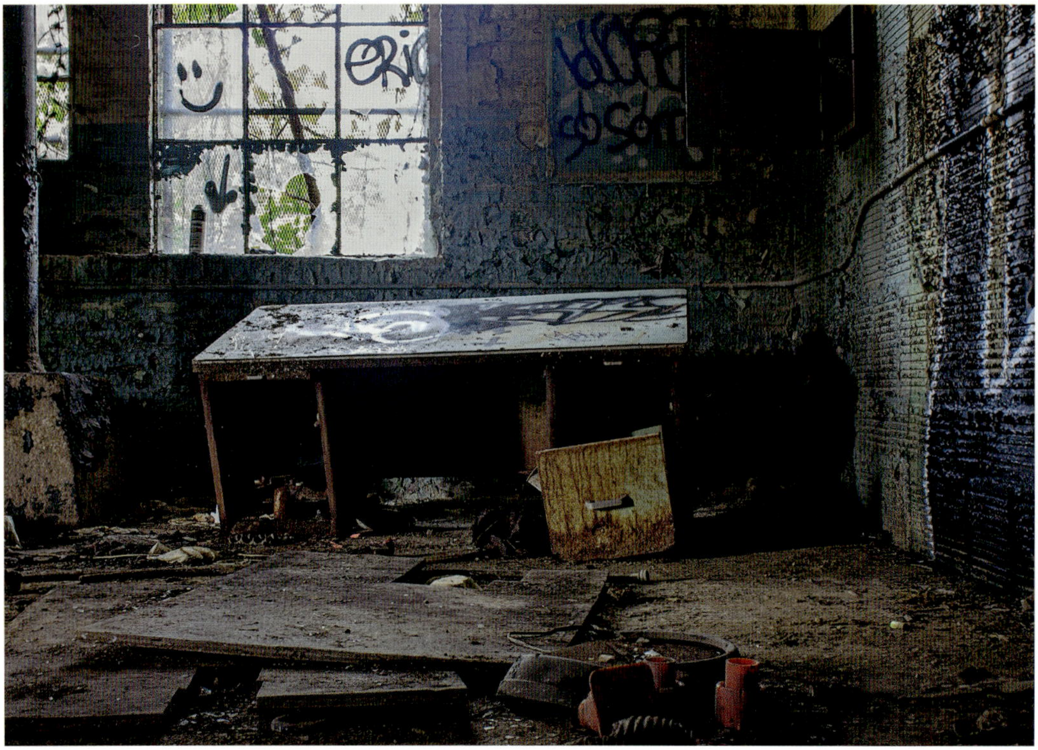

The office and admin building of Fulton Gas Works.

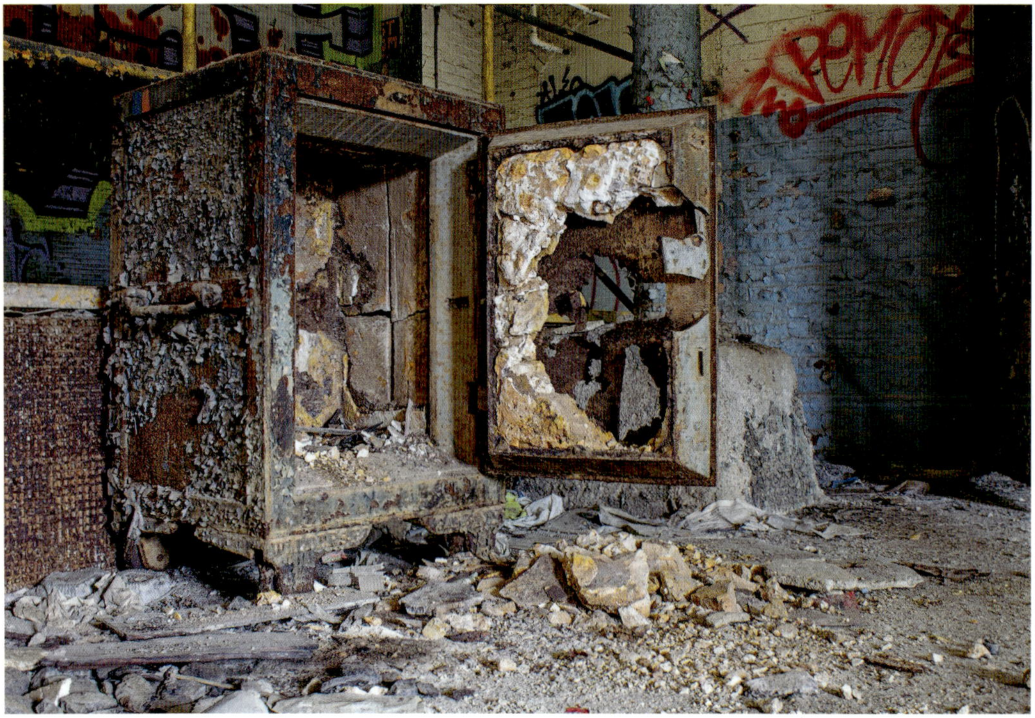

A rusted-out empty safe remains.

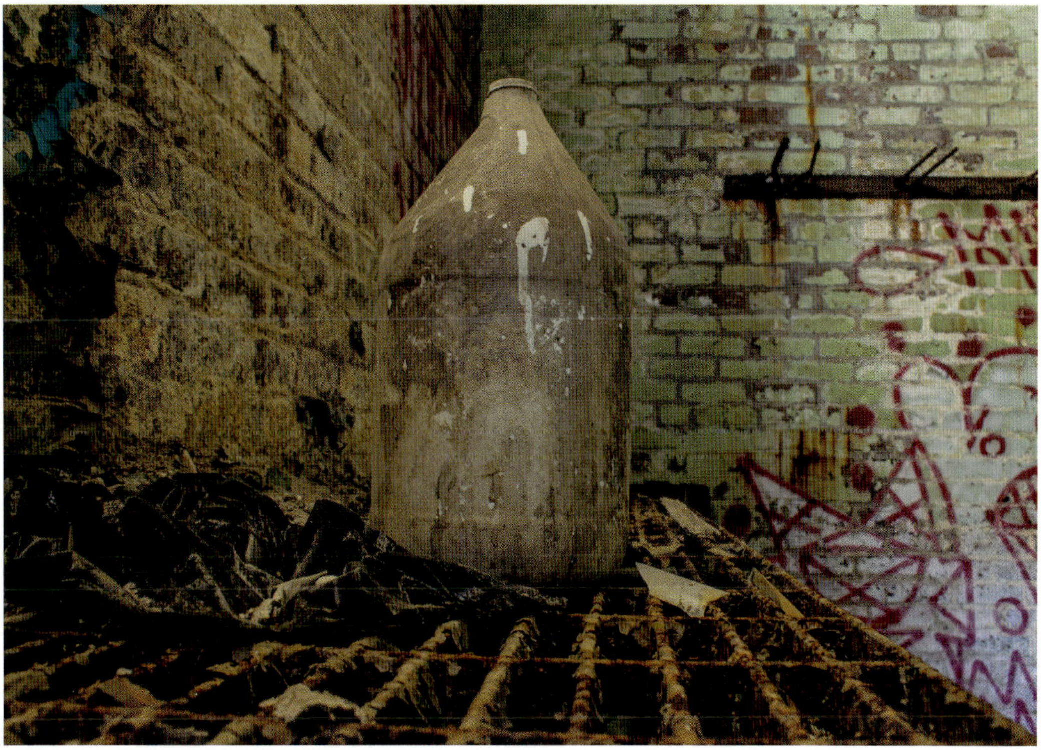

Supplies left over in one of the rooms.

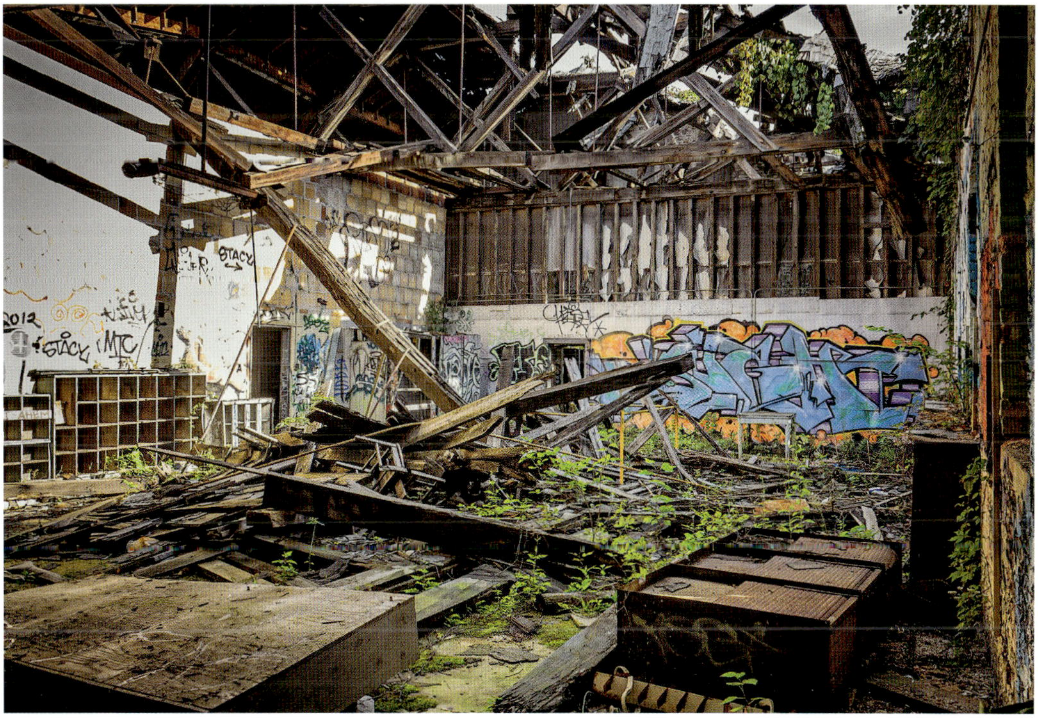

The employee area upstairs sprouts new life.

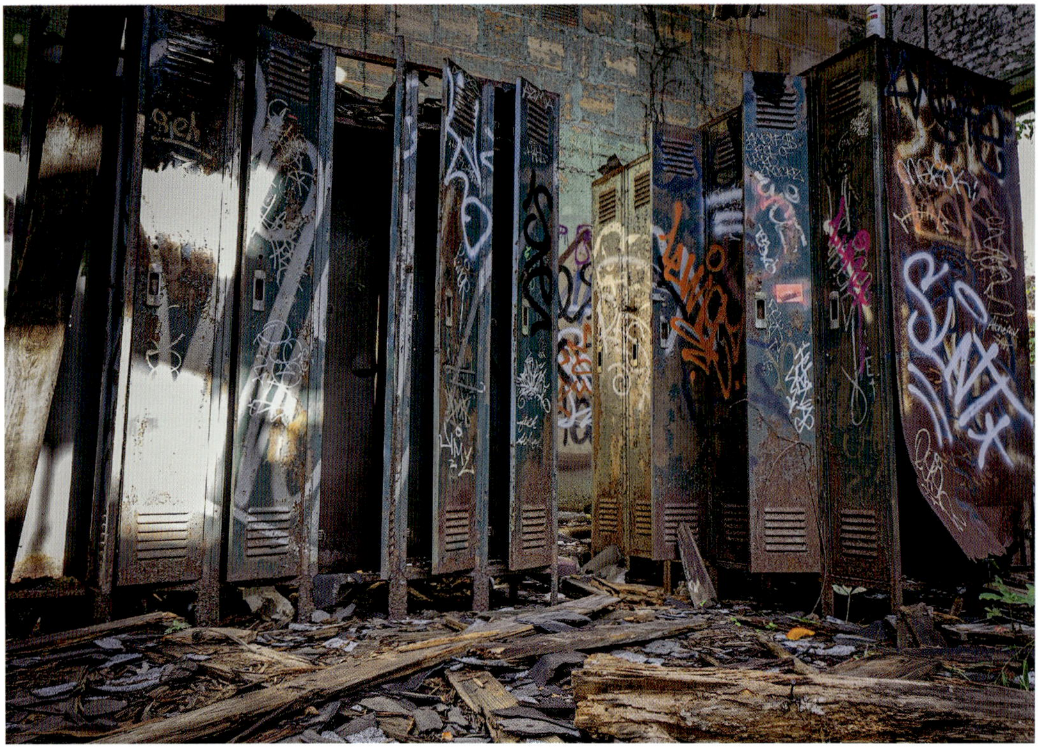

Employee lockers in the breakroom at Fulton Gas.

The City of Richmond adopted an ordinance in 1848 that created the Committee on Light, which was tasked for finding suitable methods for the manufacture and distribution of carbureted hydrogen gas from bituminous coal for the purpose of illumination of the streets, lanes, and alleys of the city. Operations began on the site in 1851. Located in the heart of the city with no room for expansion, the committee recommended the purchase of the current site of Fulton Gas Works in the Fulton neighborhood where there was room to expand. The land was purchased in 1853 and construction began immediately. Fulton Gas Works took over manufactured gas production for the city in October 1856. Over the years, it was used for several different types of fuels until its closure in the 1970s. Currently, the City of Richmond has plans to restore the grounds and repurpose the land.

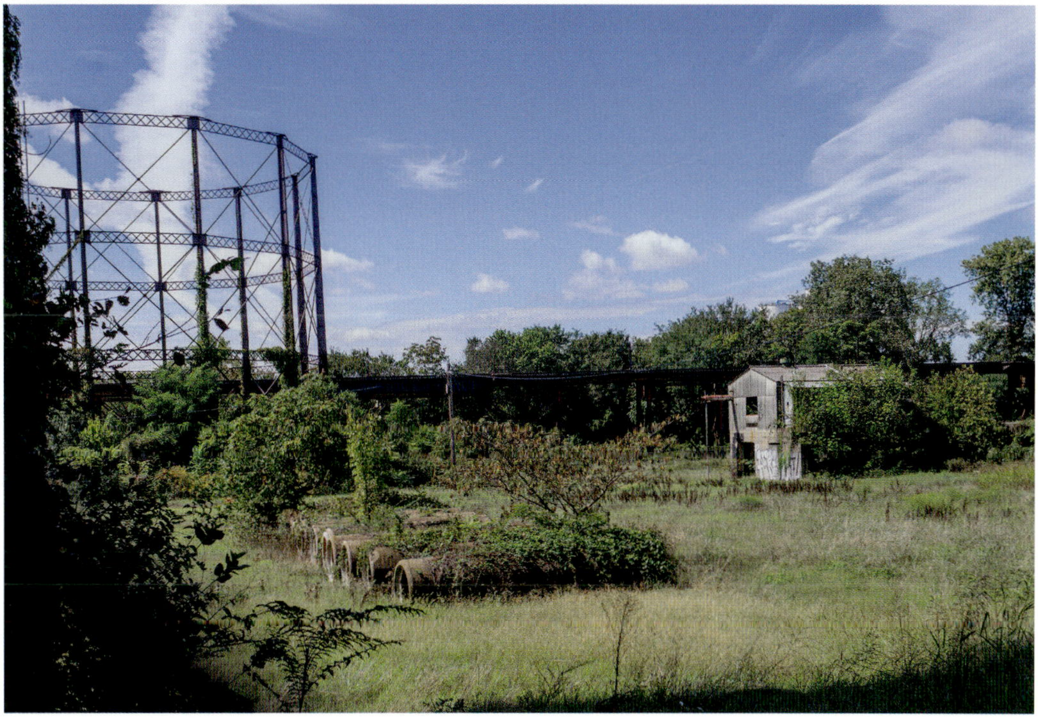

A view of the grounds at Fulton Gas Works.

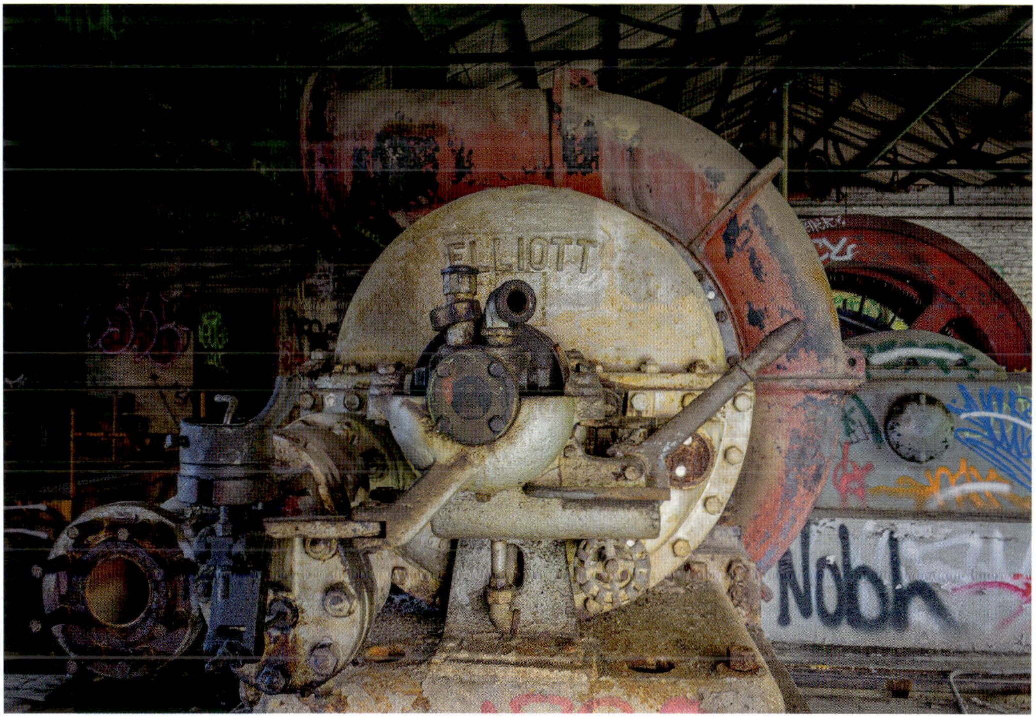

Machinery at Gas Fulton Works has been covered in graffiti.

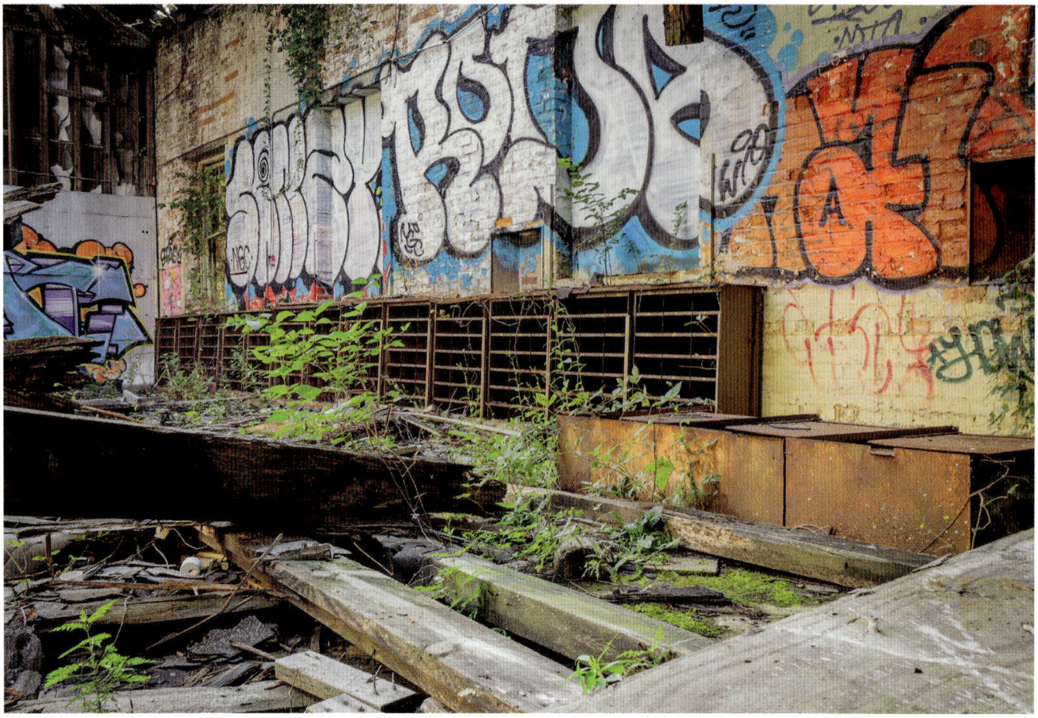

Another view of the employee bins.

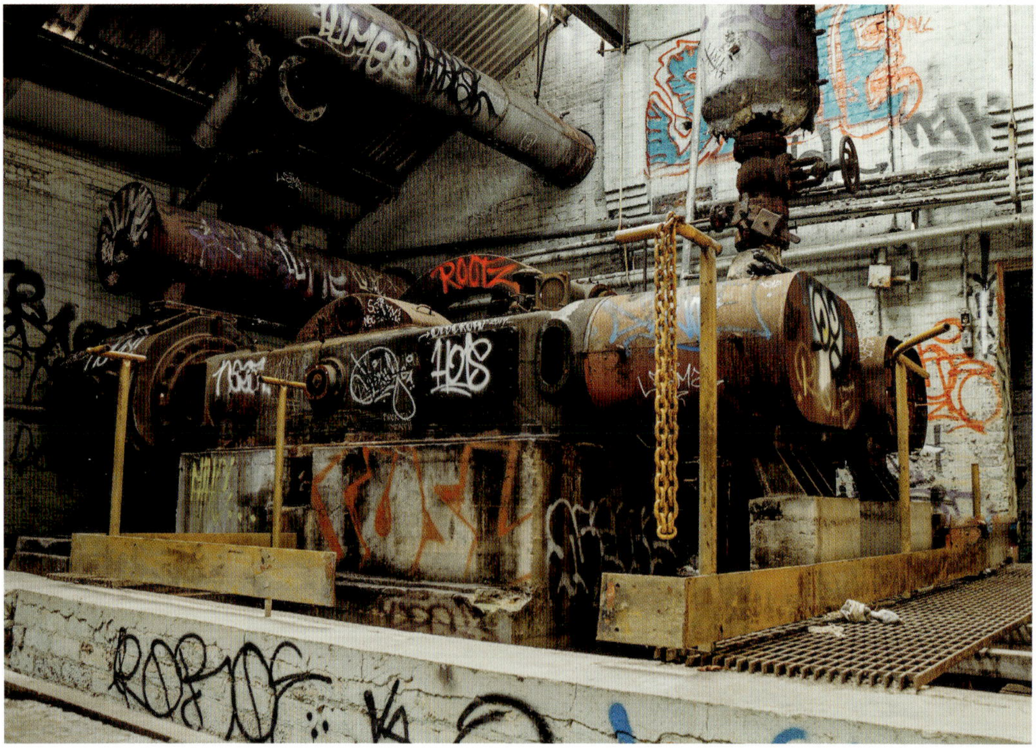

Heavy machinery at Fulton Gas Works.

6

"THE HILL" – LORTON REFORMATORY

Where Only the Strong Survived

Lorton Reformatory has a very notorious past, and at one time was the main prison for the District of Columbia. Also known as Occoquan Workhouse, it sat on 1,100 acres and even had its own railroad up until the 1970s. The penitentiary buildings of the 1930s were constructed by the prisoners themselves, using brick manufactured at the on-site kiln complex from Occoquan River clay. Notable inmates of the prison included famous musician Chuck Brown, Lucy Burns, Petey Green, Laura Houghtaling Ingalls, and FBI agent George Gordon Liddy.

During the 1960s, prominent national suffragists were arrested from their "Silent Sentinels" pickets at the White House and held at the Occoquan Workhouse. Approximately 168 women were mistreated at the workhouse. Some women were force-fed after they began hunger strikes. November 14, 1917, is known as the "Night of Terror" because of how badly these suffragist prisoners were tortured, beaten, and abused.

This prison was known as a place where "only the strong survived." It was arguably one of the most corrupt prison systems of its time, with stories from inmates that are almost hard to believe. These stories include tales of family members that were guards (which gave inmates access to almost anything they wanted, including weapons and drugs), prostitution (including the female guards), corrupt guards, and a high murder rate.

The Lorton Reformatory was closed in 1999, and the last prisoners were removed in late 2001. Today, many of the former prison buildings have been turned into swanky homes, a museum, and retail space.

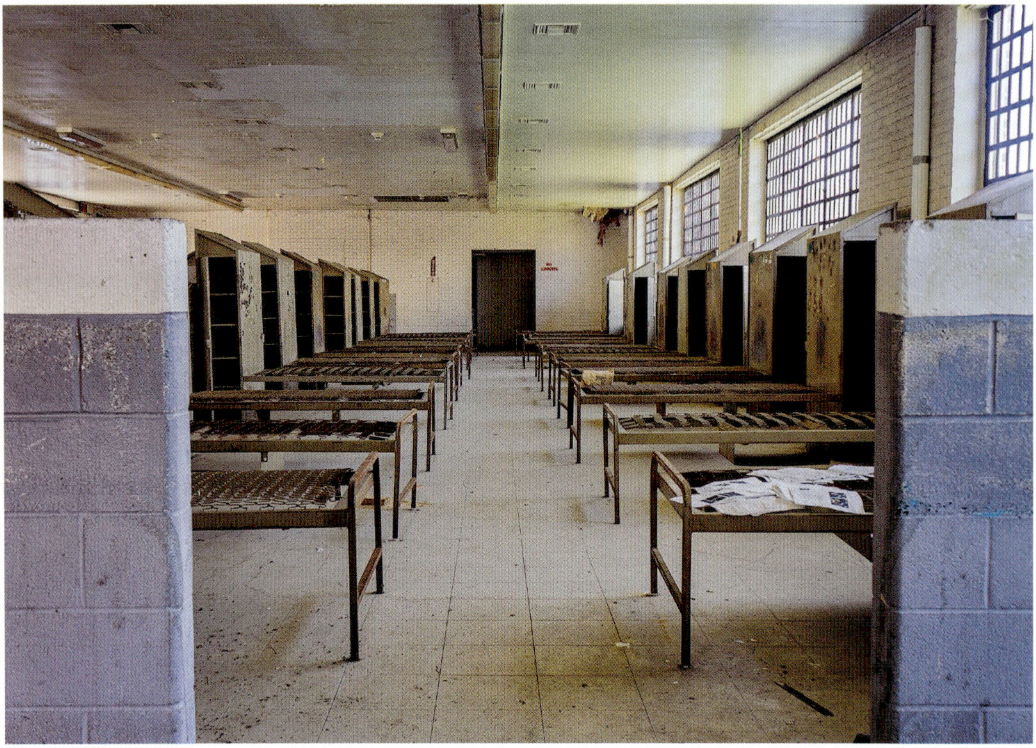

Beds and lockers in Lorton Reformatory.

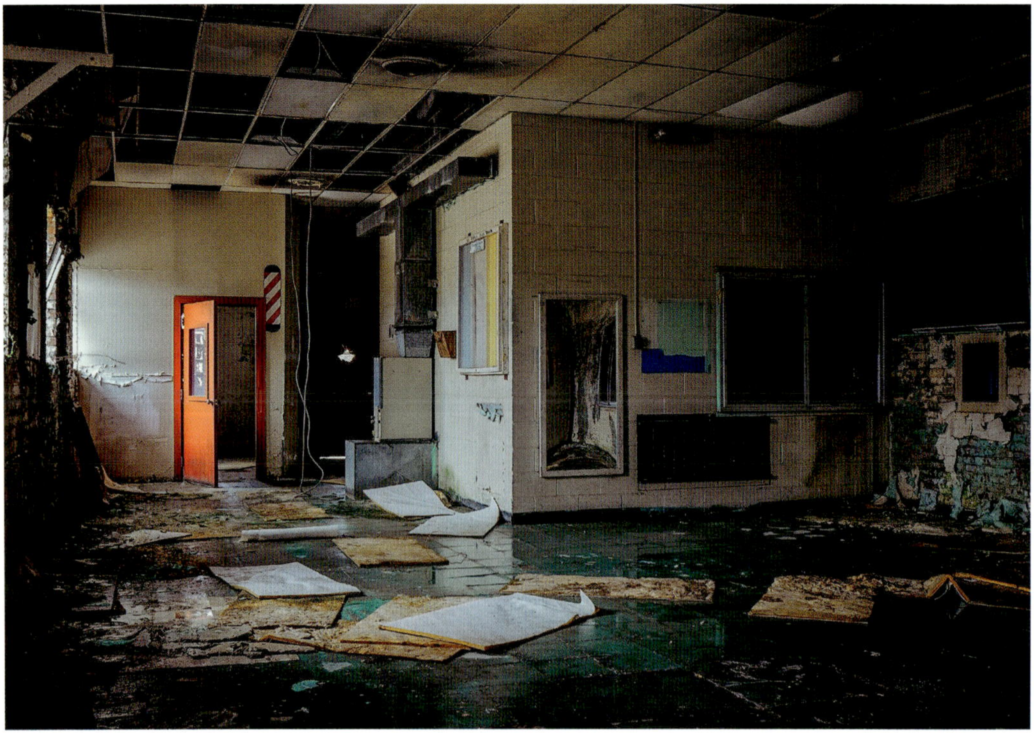

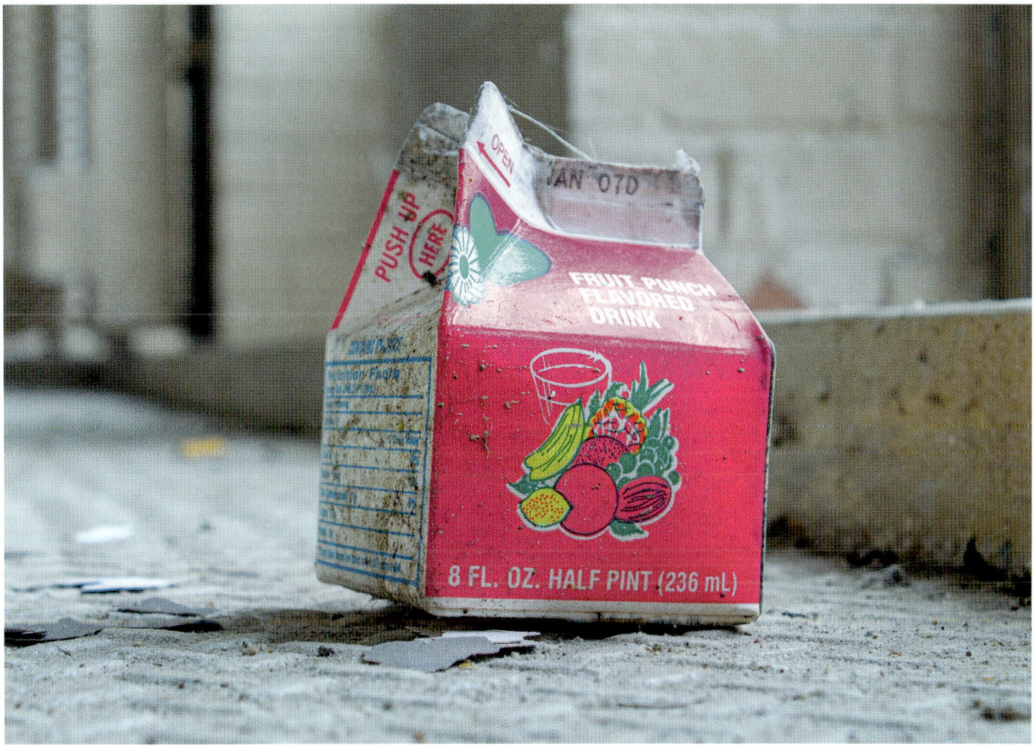

Milk carton left in one of the bunks.

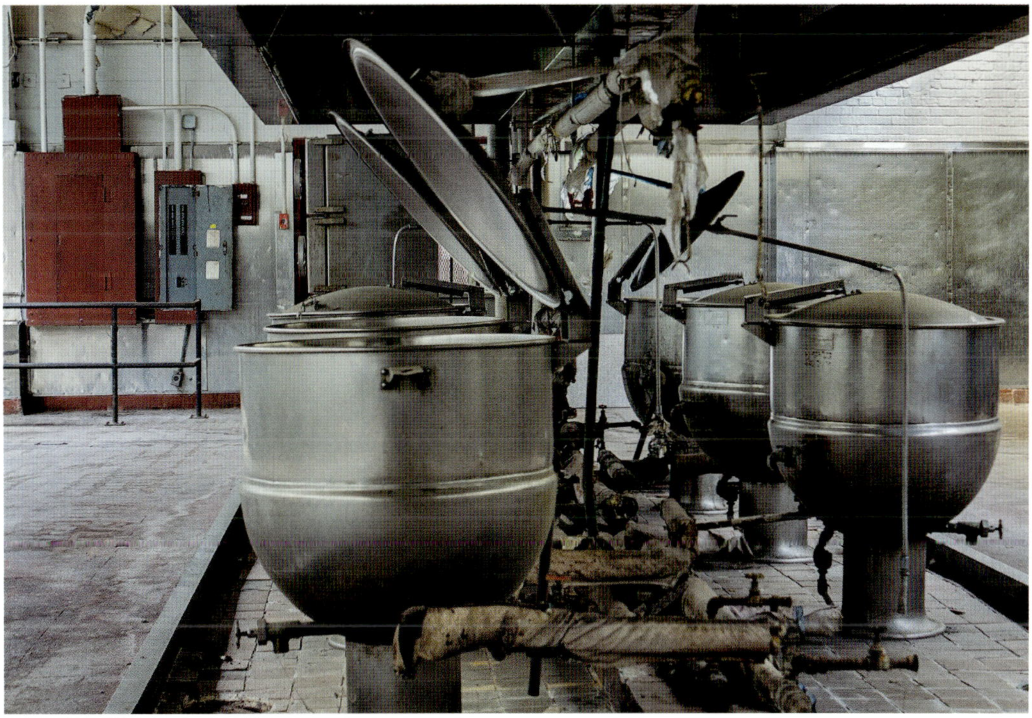

Kitchen machinery at Lorton Reformatory.

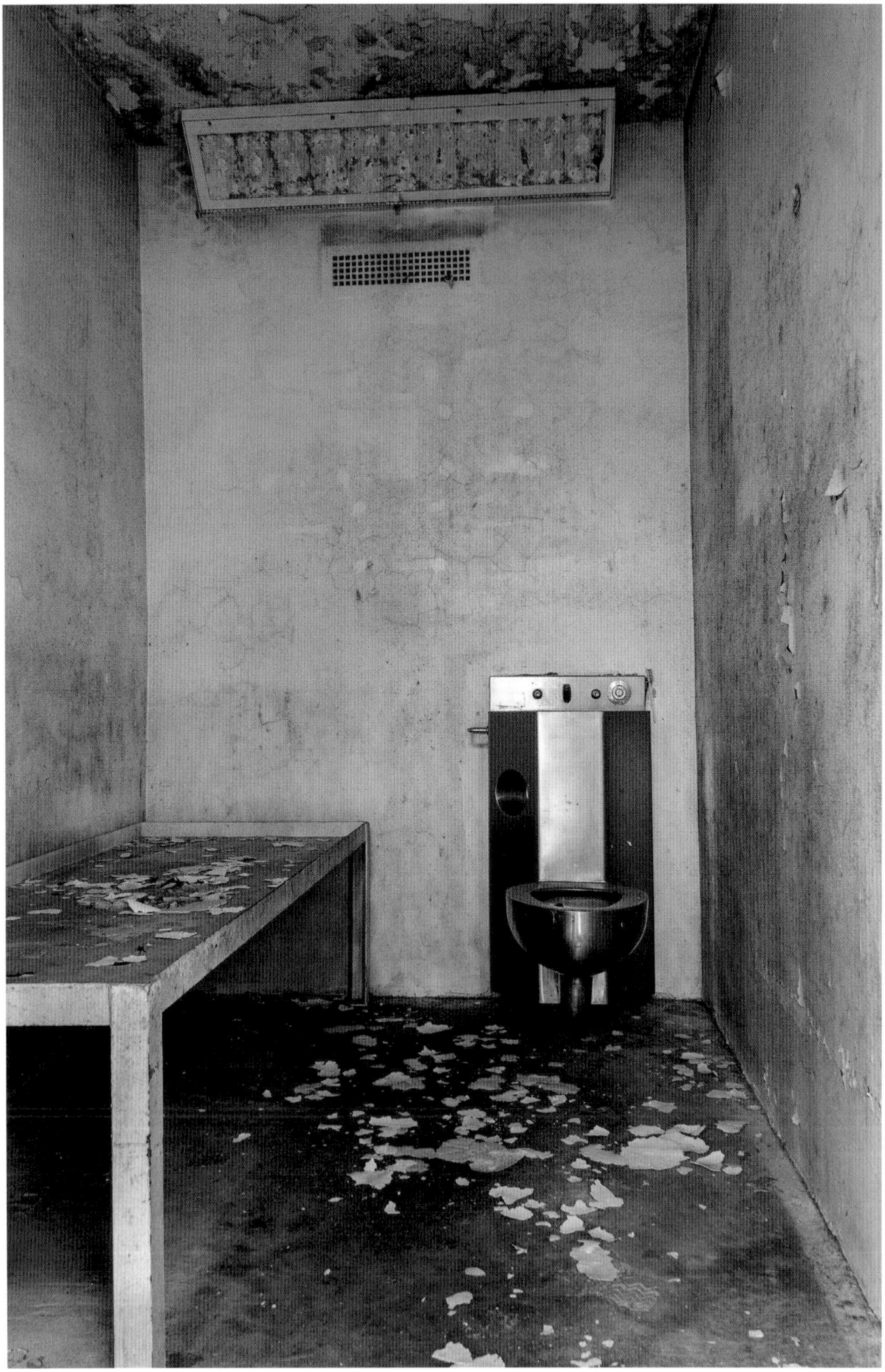

A look at the interior of a cell.

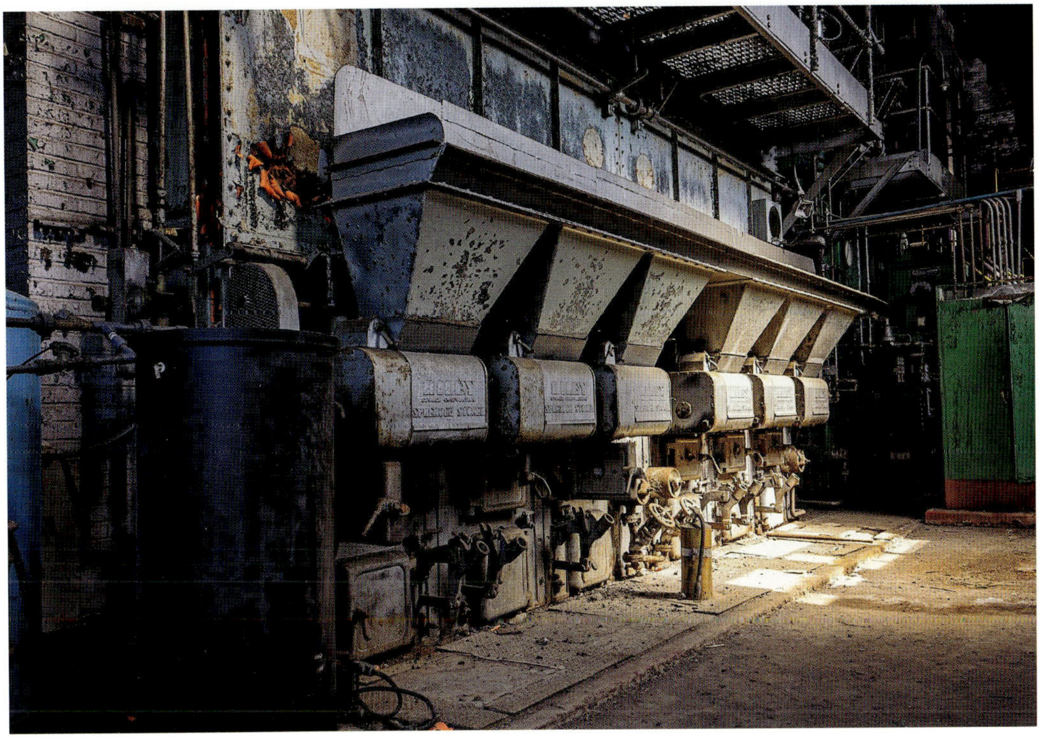

The power plant that ran the Lorton Reformatory complex.

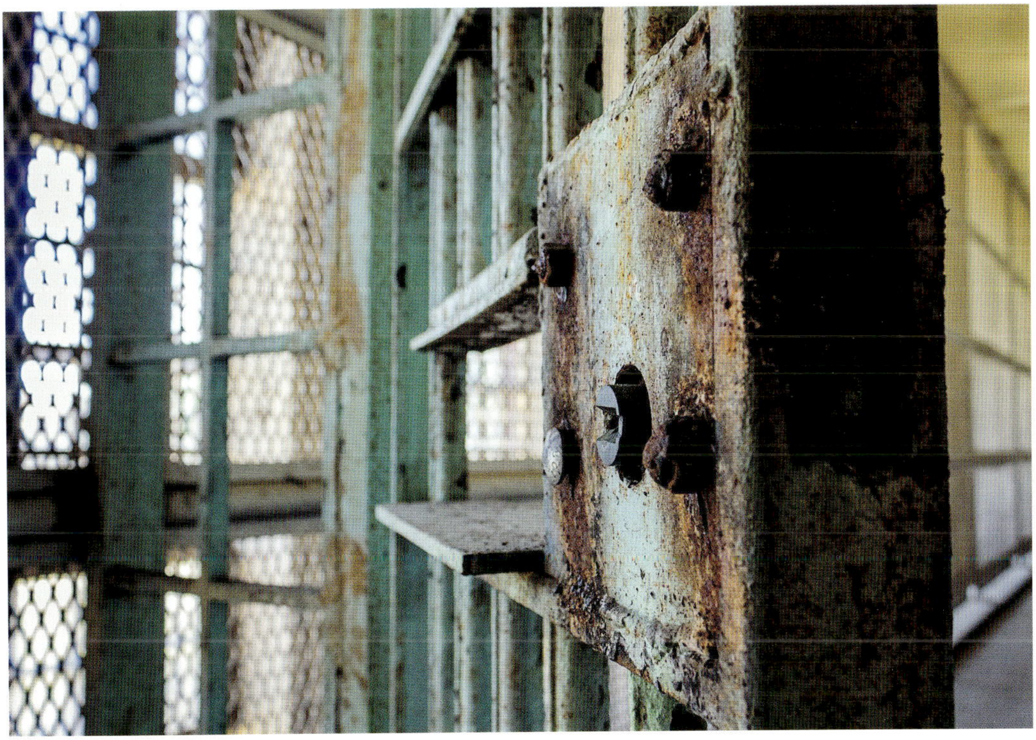

Cell door on the maximum-security wing.

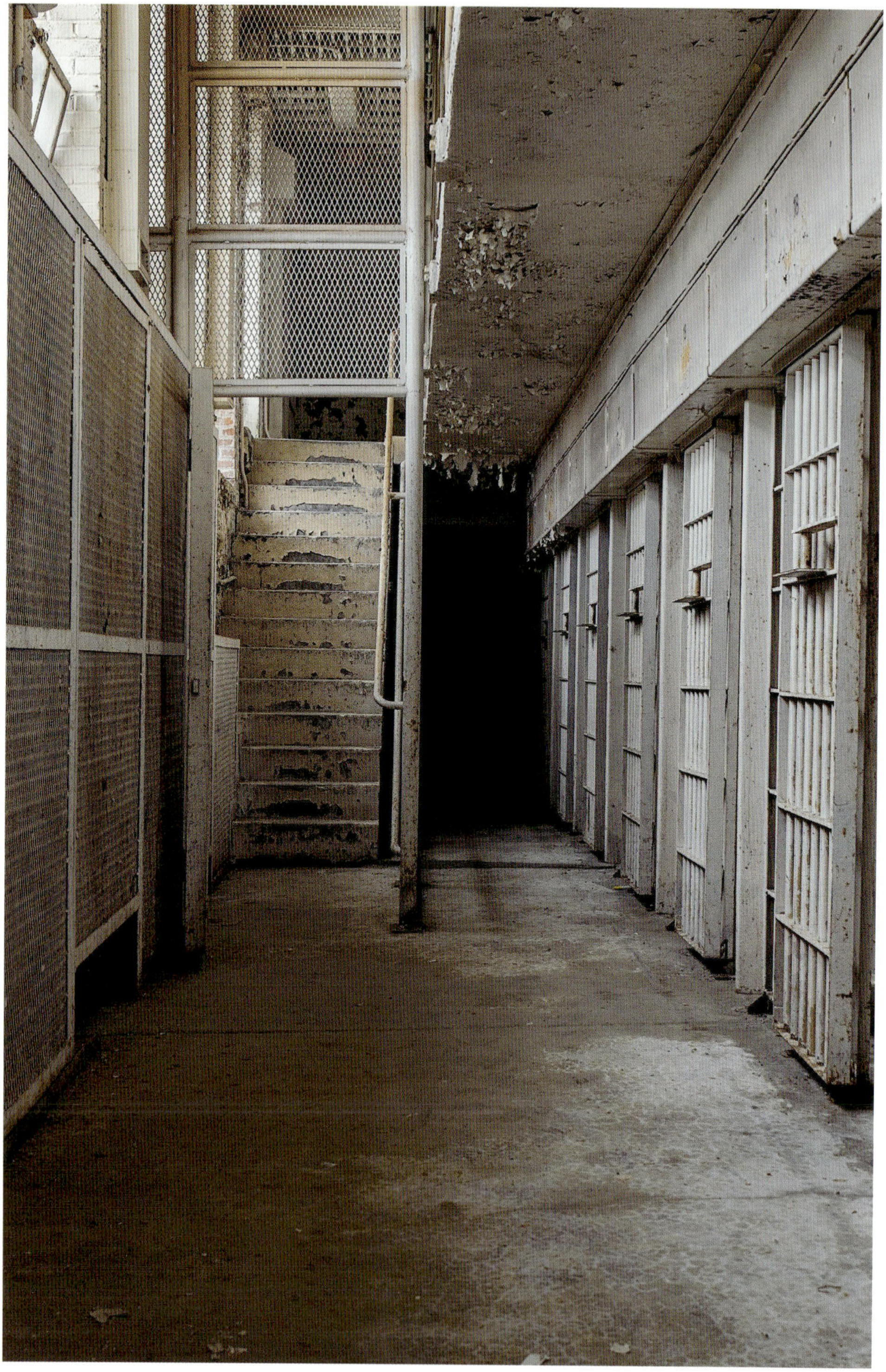

Stairs leading up to the guard catwalk.

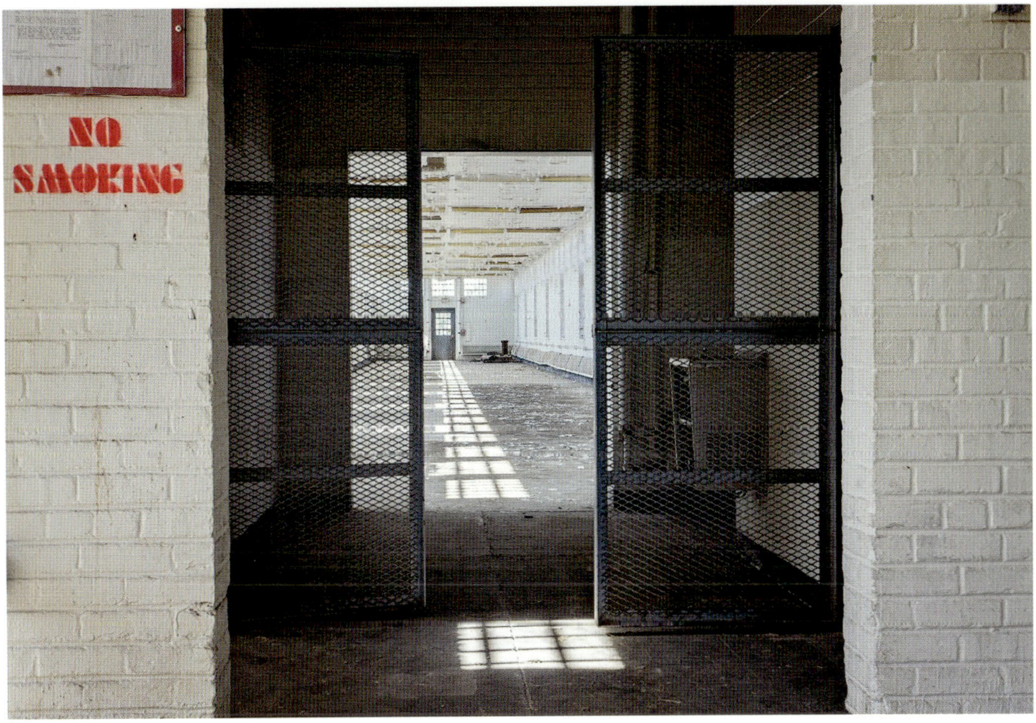

Security gates inside the prison.

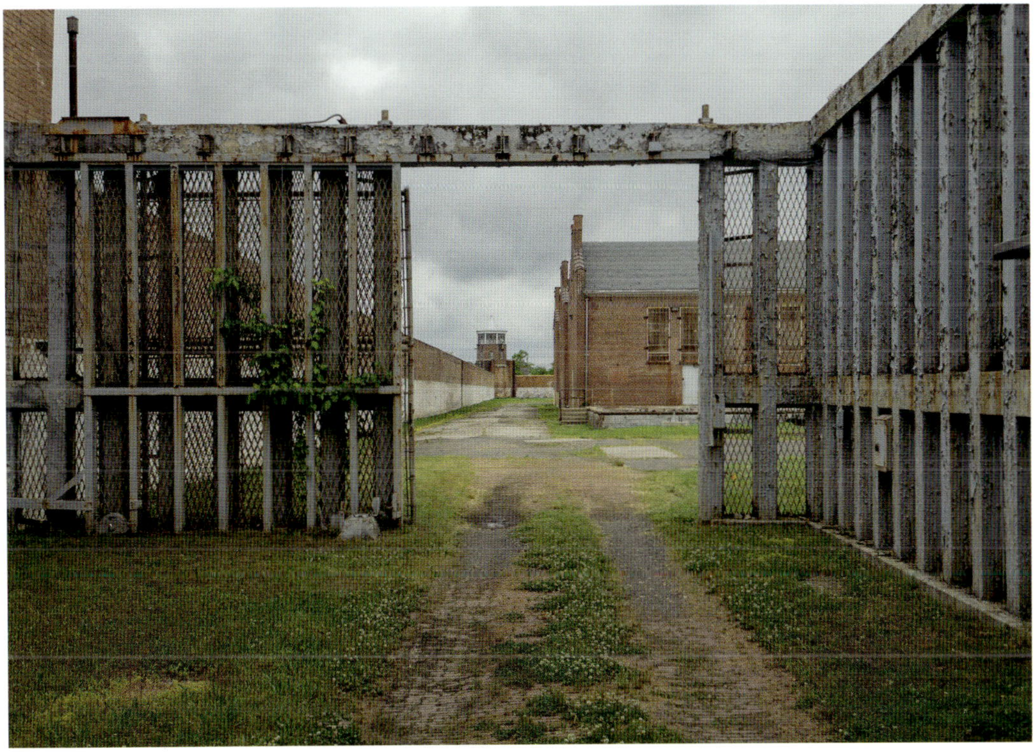

The main entrance in the maximum-security section of the prison.

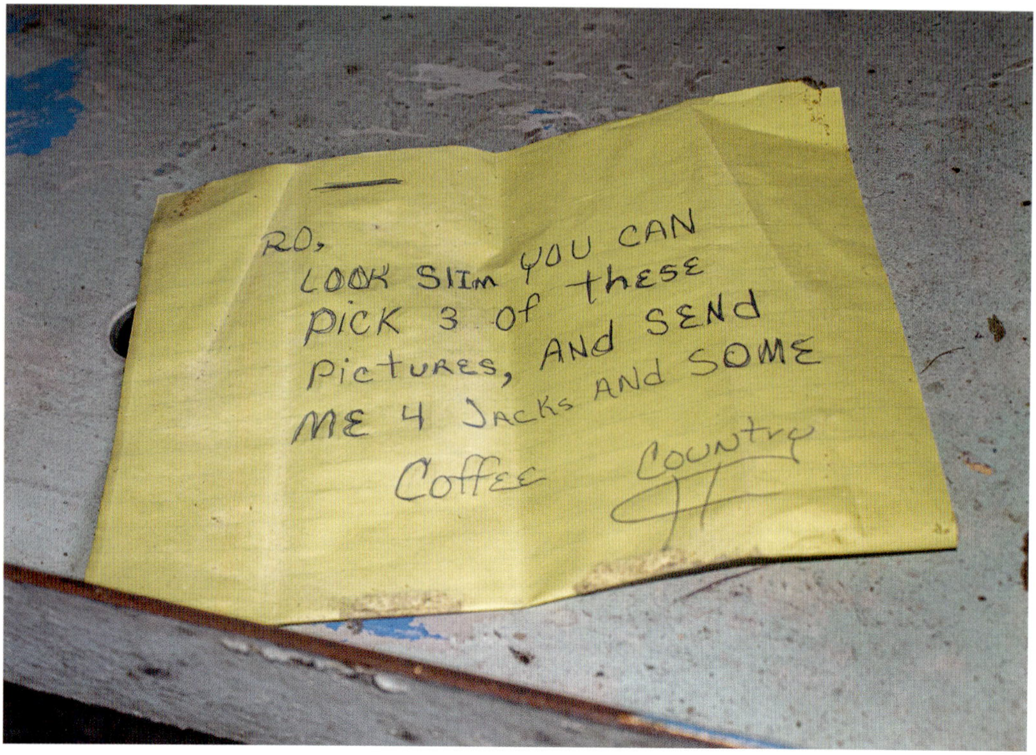

A note from one inmate to another about trading items.

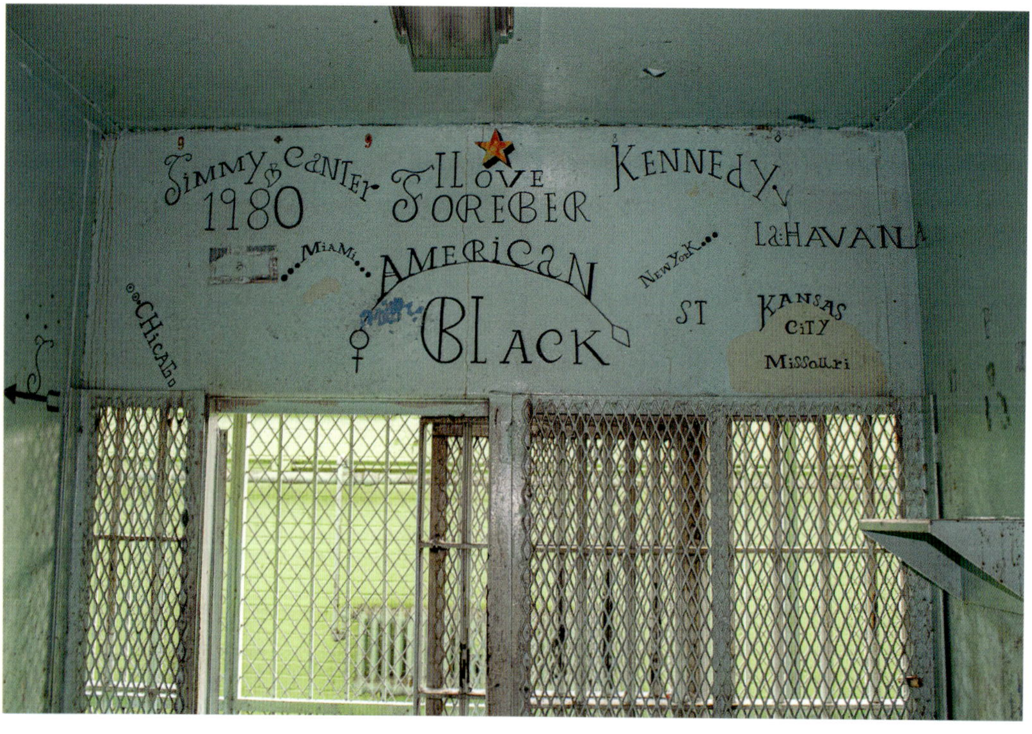

Gang graffiti writing done by the inmates.

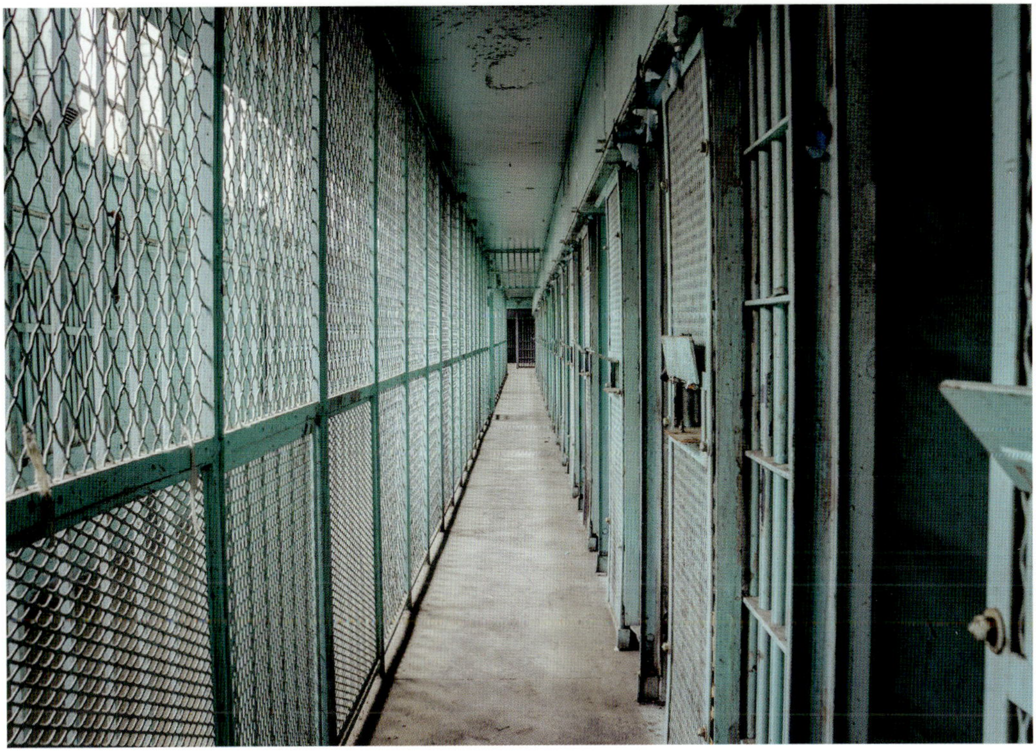

A look down the walkway outside the prisoners' cells.

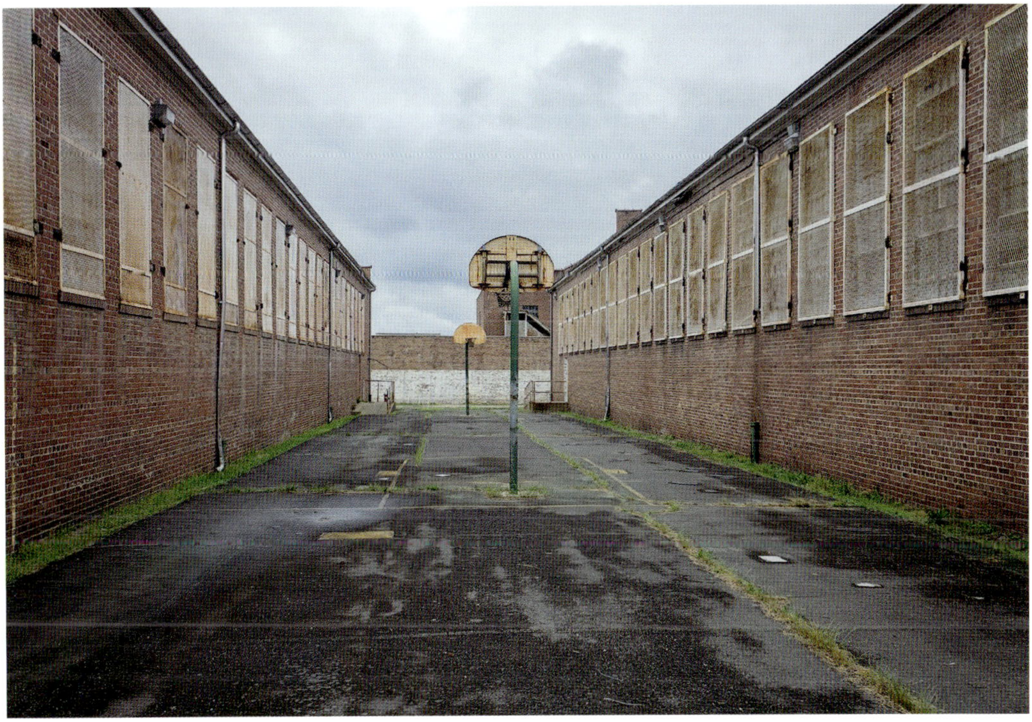

One of the basketball courts outside the dorms.

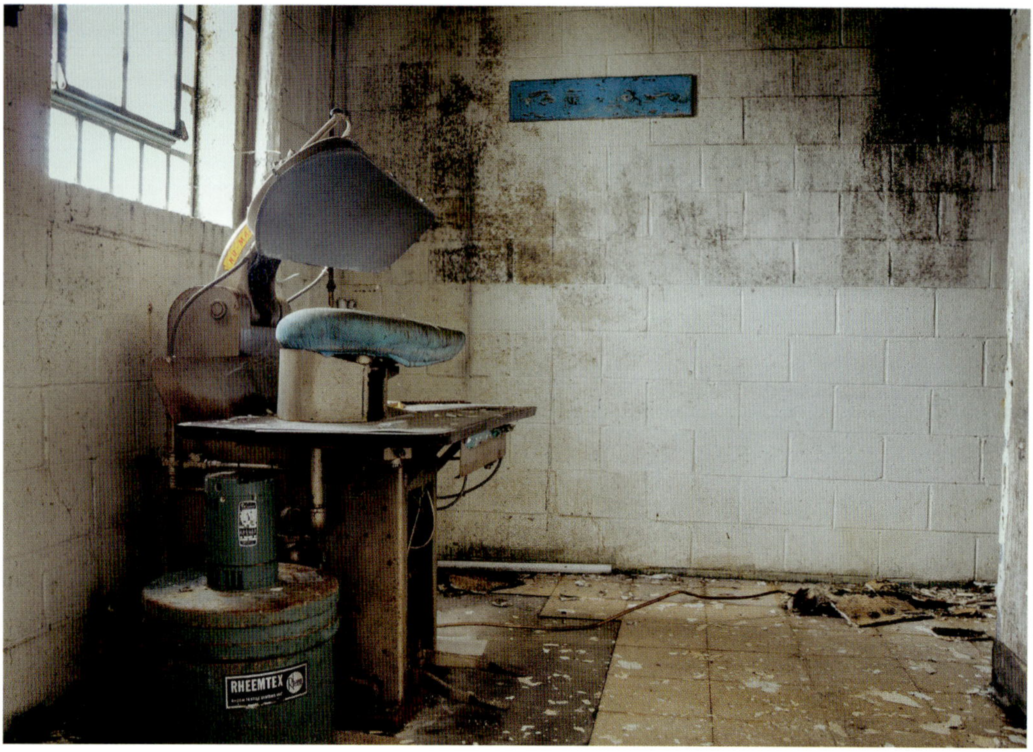

Laundry press left behind.

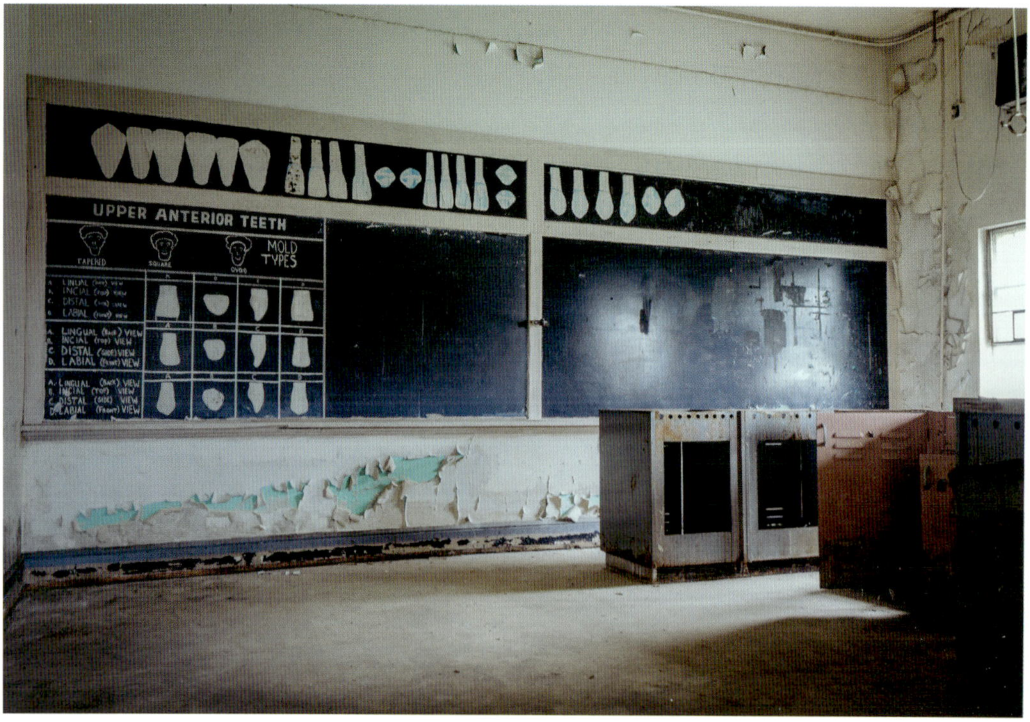

The dental office at Lorton Reformatory, complete with charts.

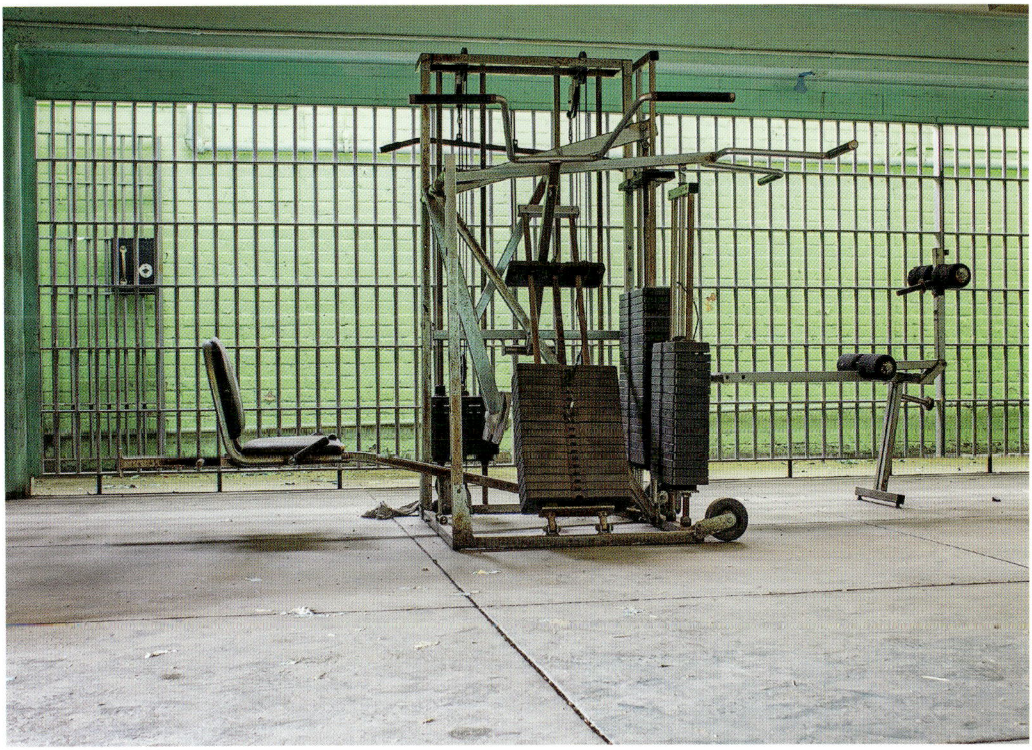

Workout station in the gym area of one dorm building.

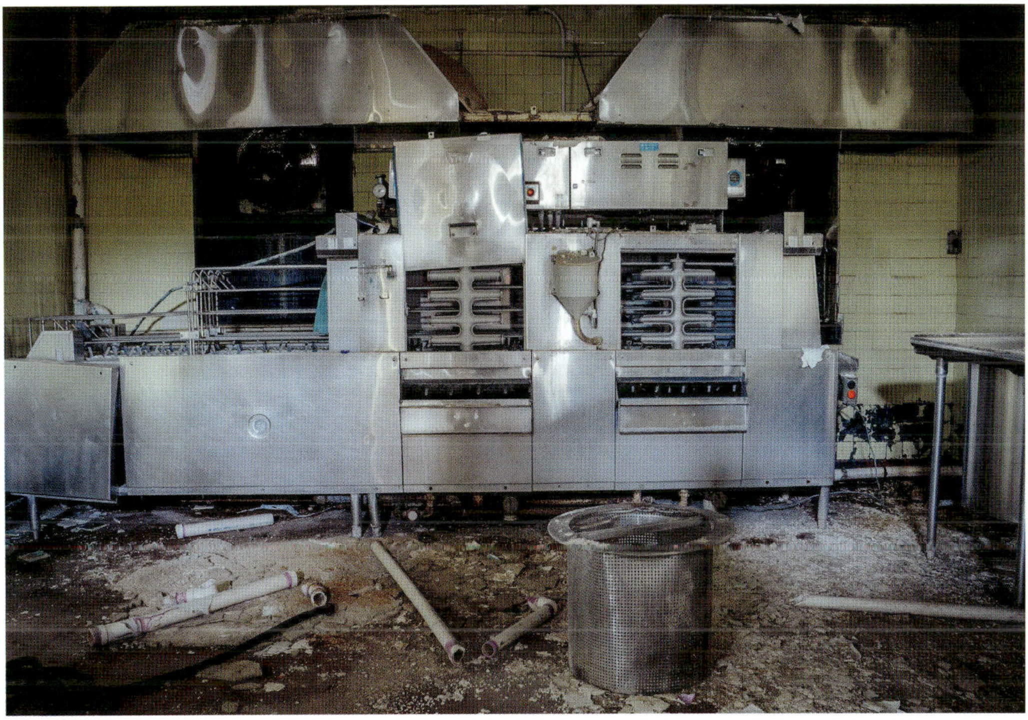

A look at the dishwasher in the kitchen.

7

ABANDONED CHURCHES

The Bible Belt is commonly regarded as an area in the Southern United States where religion has a particularly strong influence on social and political roles in their communities. While it is not an exact defined area, the Bible Belt is generally thought to include almost all of the Southeastern U.S., running from Virginia down to Northern Florida, and west to parts of Texas, Oklahoma, and Missouri. Over the years, many of these small community churches have been abandoned along with their towns as the population dwindles.

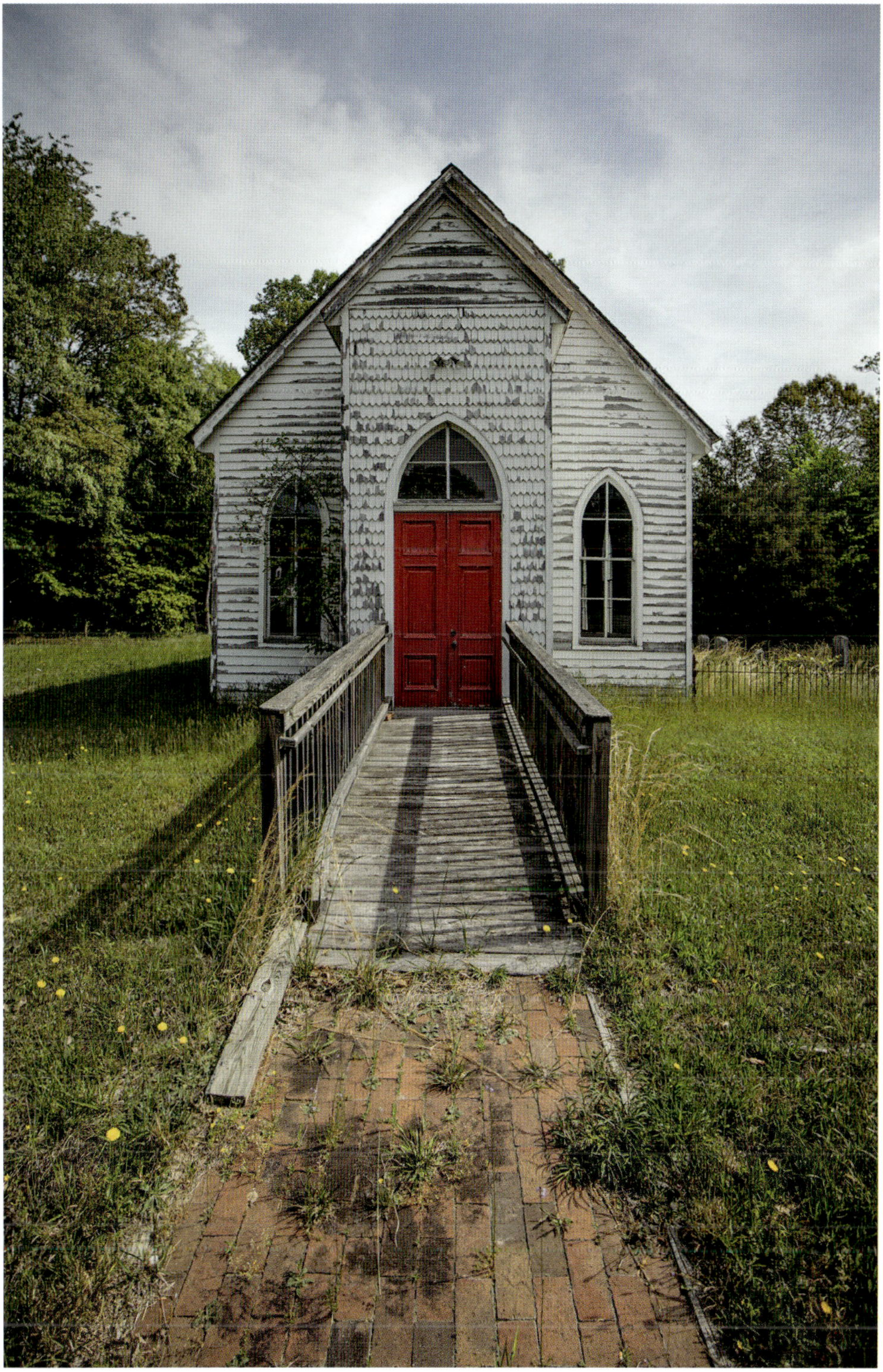

A country church sits abandoned after a new, bigger church was built.

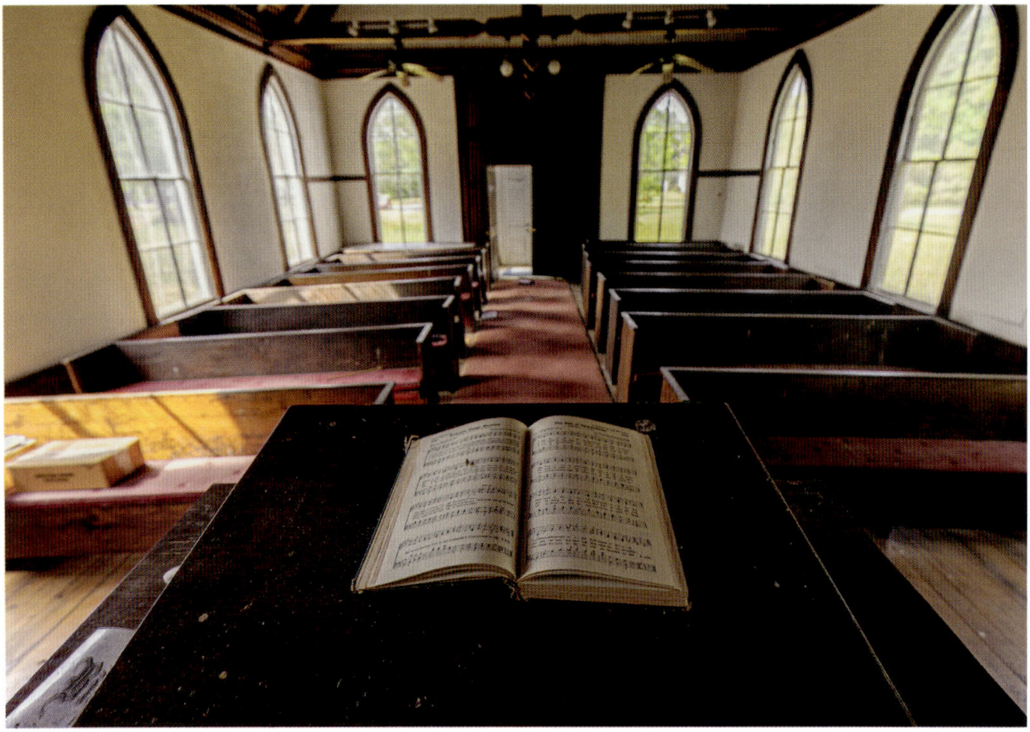

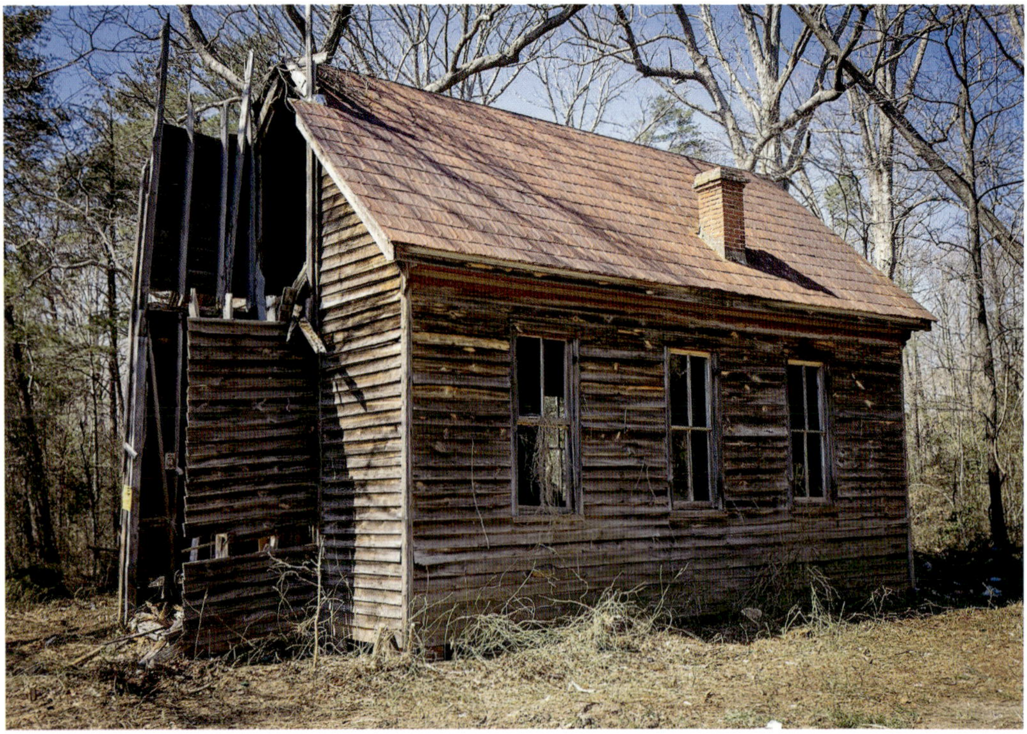

A small one-room rural church deteriorates over the years.

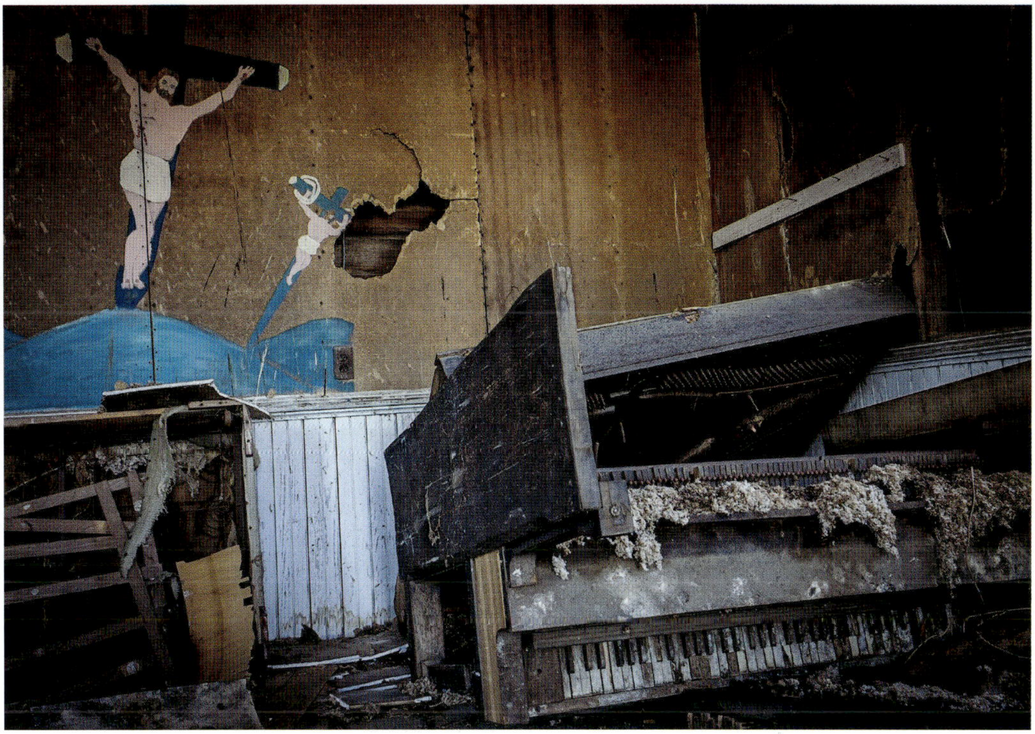

The inside of the church with hand drawn paintings on the walls.

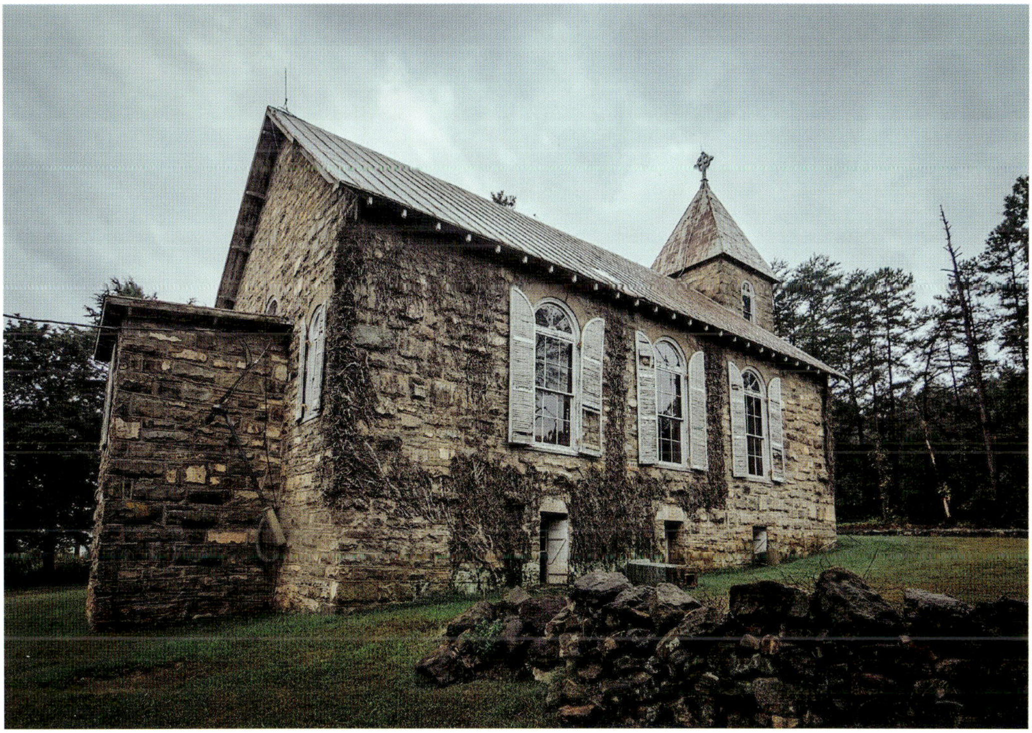

A historical local church in central Virginia.

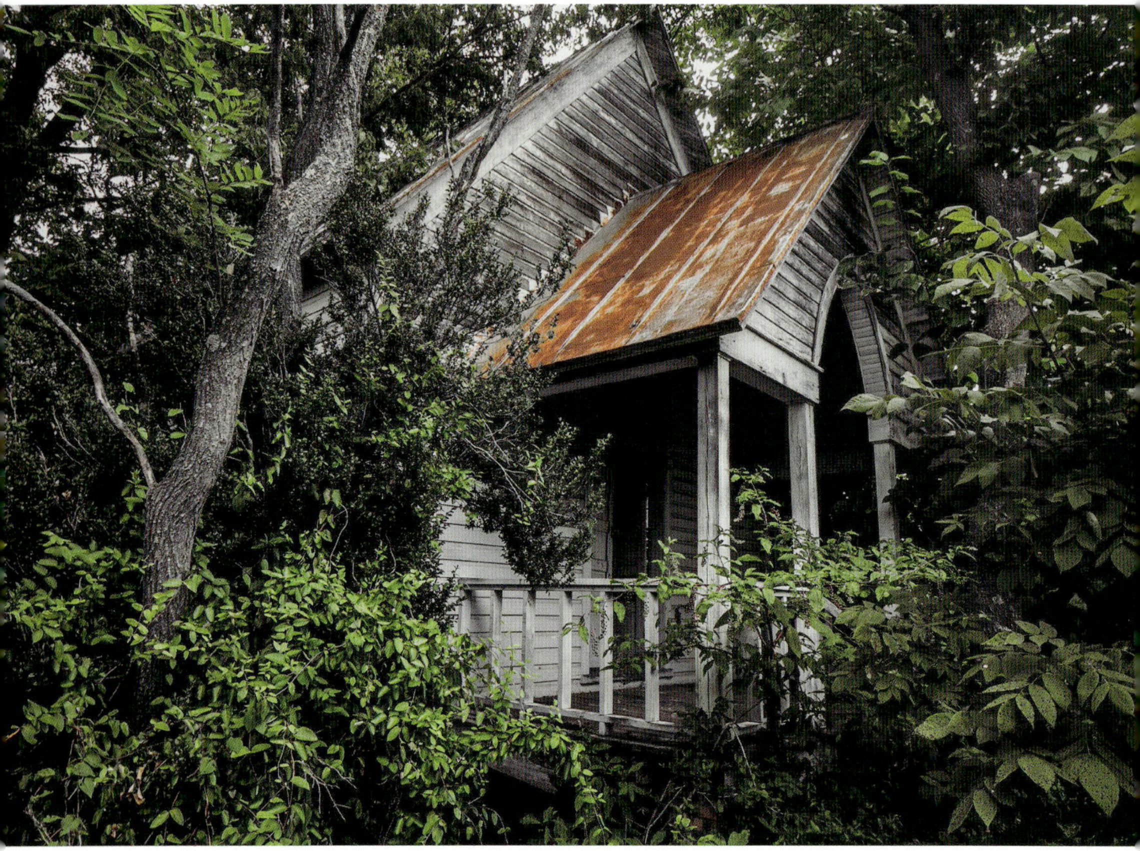

This country church is slowly being covered by vegetation. It's barely visible in summer months.

8

DEATH OF THE SMALL-TOWN BUSINESS

The Interstate System, which was created by President Eisenhower as the Federal-Aid Highway Act of 1956, changed the landscape of America in many ways. The new system of major roadways sped up travel at the expense of many small towns and businesses. The now mostly defunct Route 66, or Mother Road, is a great example. Migration and tourism played a major part in shaping towns along Route 66, even well before the road was officially established in 1926. The creation of the Interstate Highway System destroyed many of these towns and communities when it circumvented Route 66 beginning in the late 1970s.

This ripple effect was also felt among towns and businesses in Virginia along highways such as Highway 1, and U.S Route 301. These small towns thrived economically and socially on the success of their local businesses. When the economy was doing well, other parts of the town were successful also, such as population growth and the value of housing. The downside was that driving through these small towns slowed down travelers passing through. Part of the Interstate System included highway bypasses, which were constructed to steer traffic around these towns, and in turn decreasing travel time. The result on small town communities and businesses was devastating and can still be felt today.

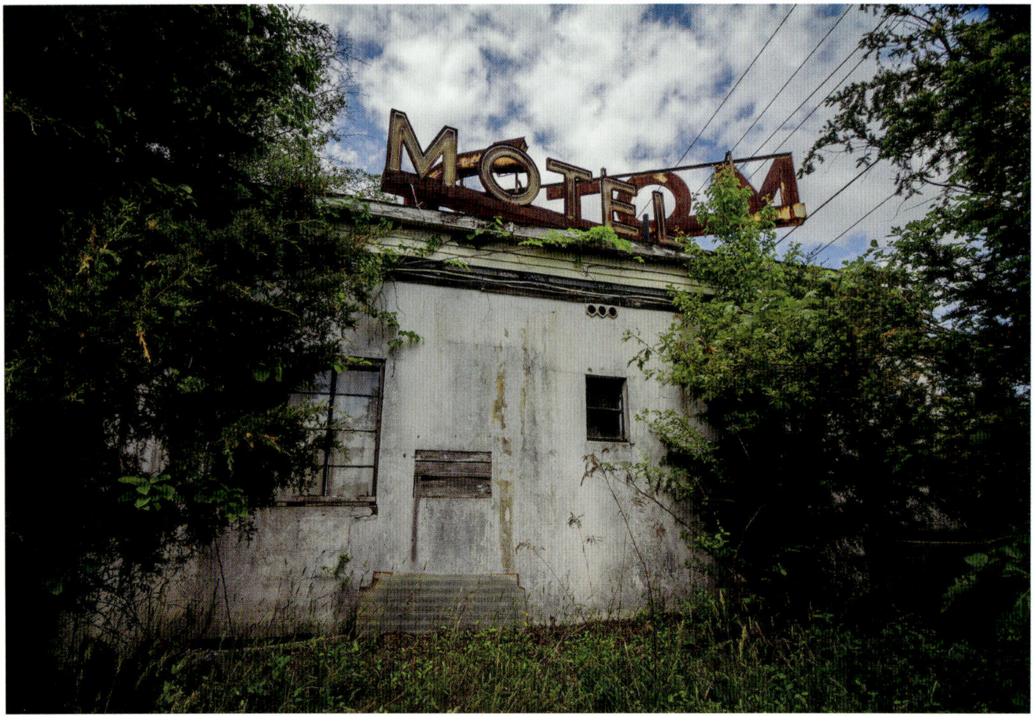

The sign atop the motel.

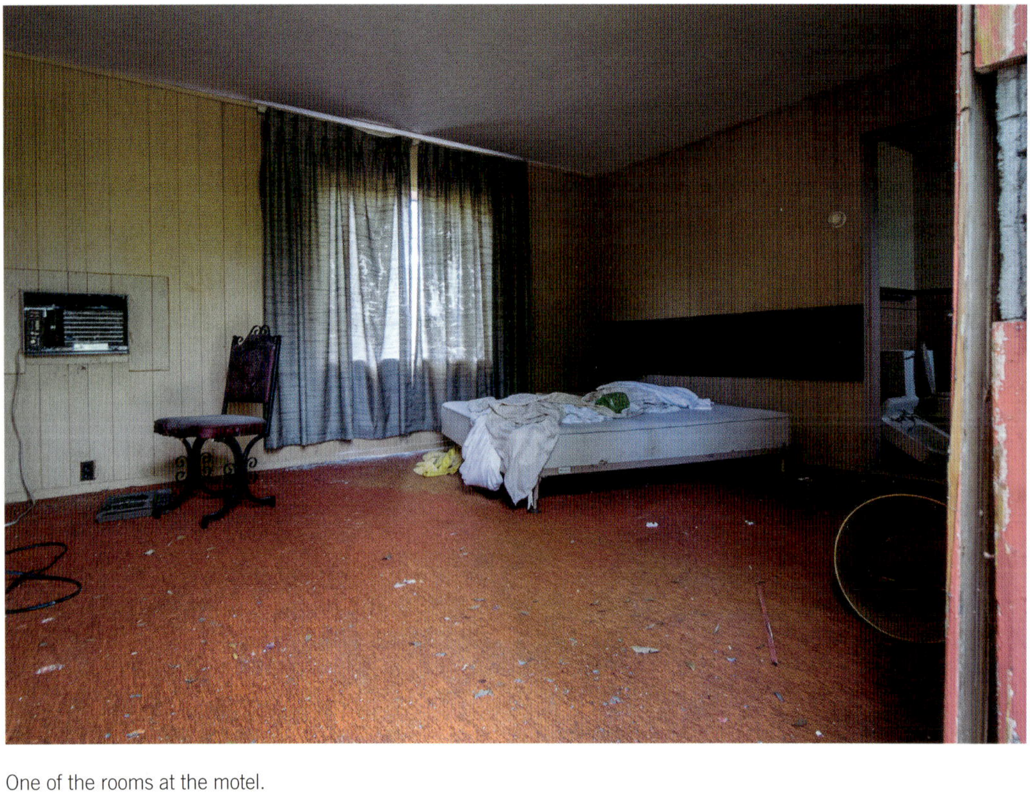

One of the rooms at the motel.

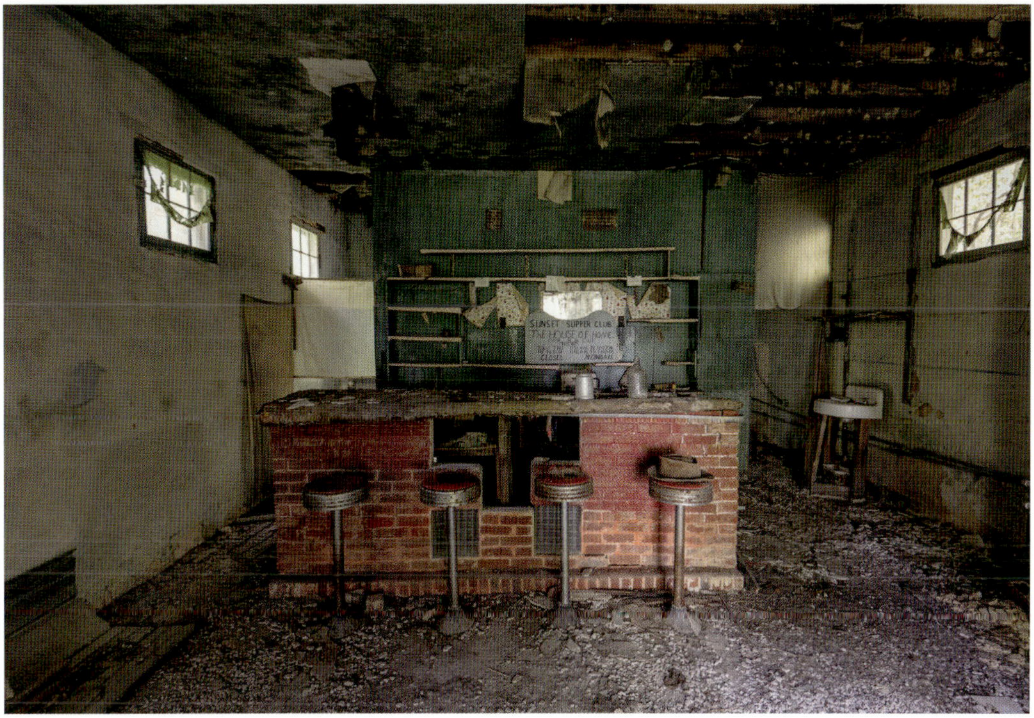

The bar at a small country diner.

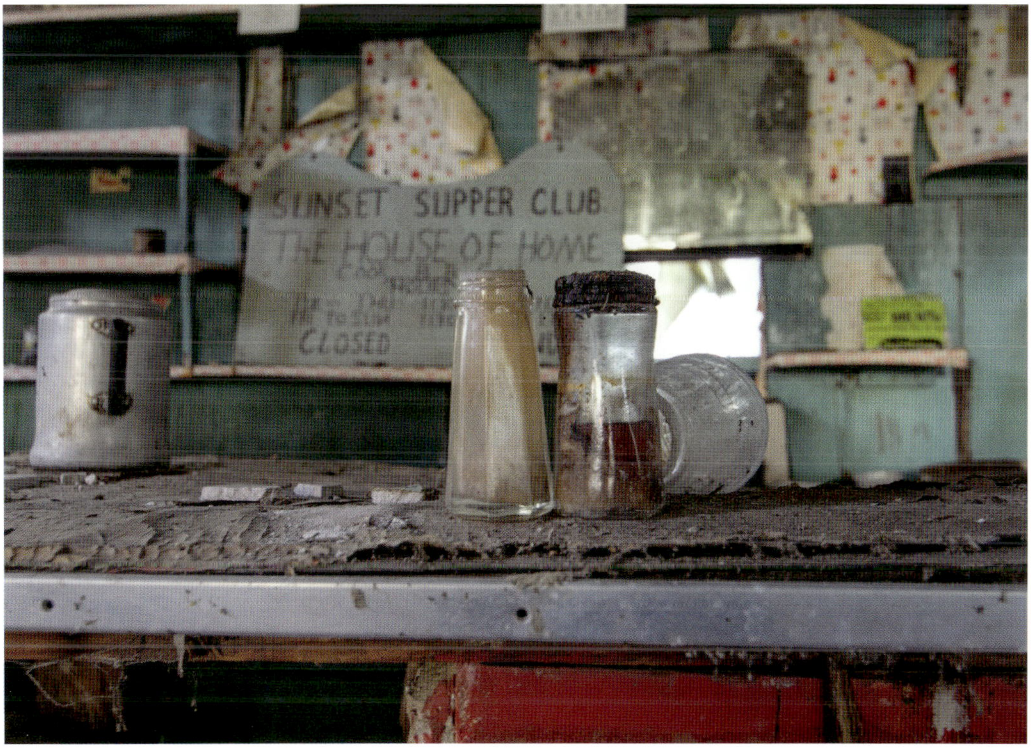

The home cooking diner was known for their fried baloney sandwiches.

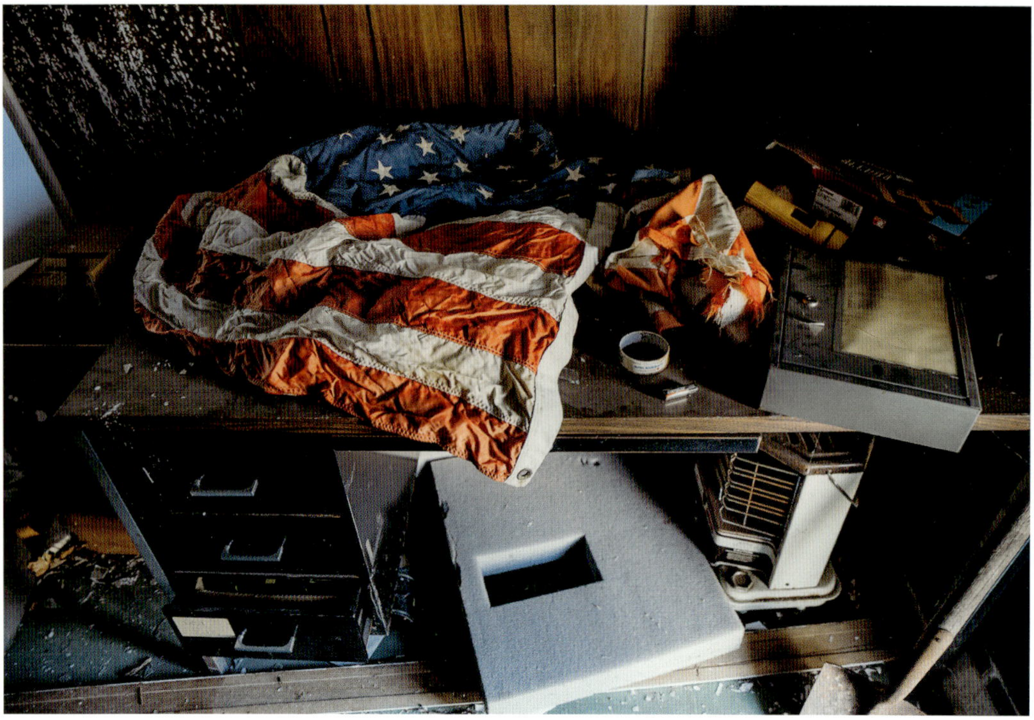

An American flag left behind in one of the office rooms.

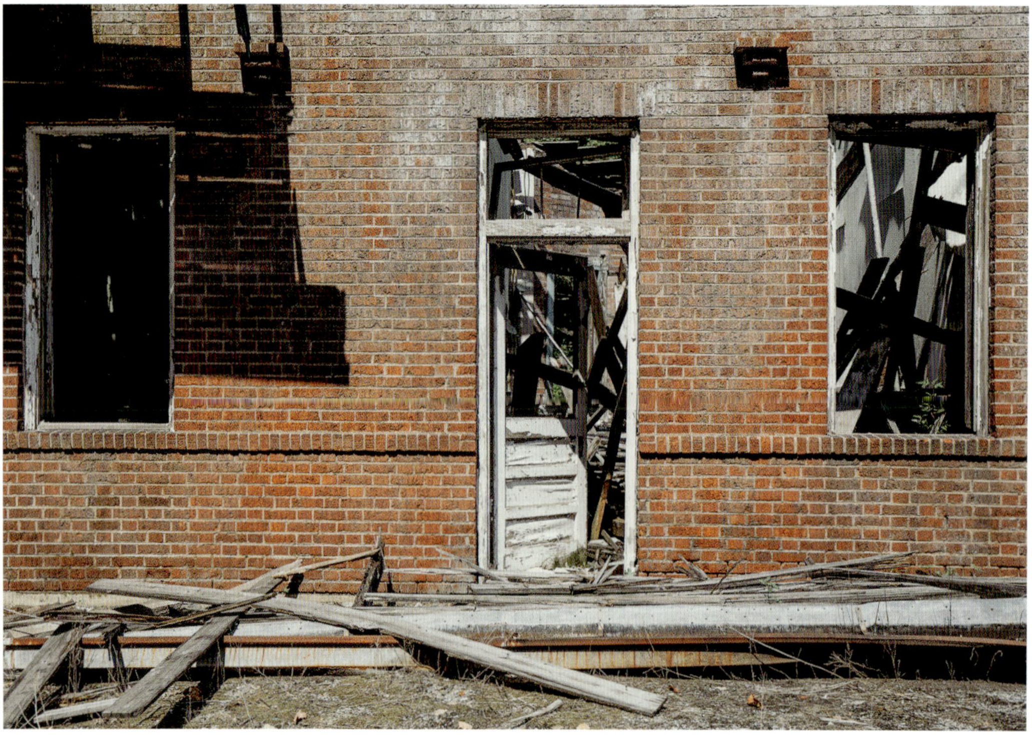

A railroad station in a once booming town that has all but died off.

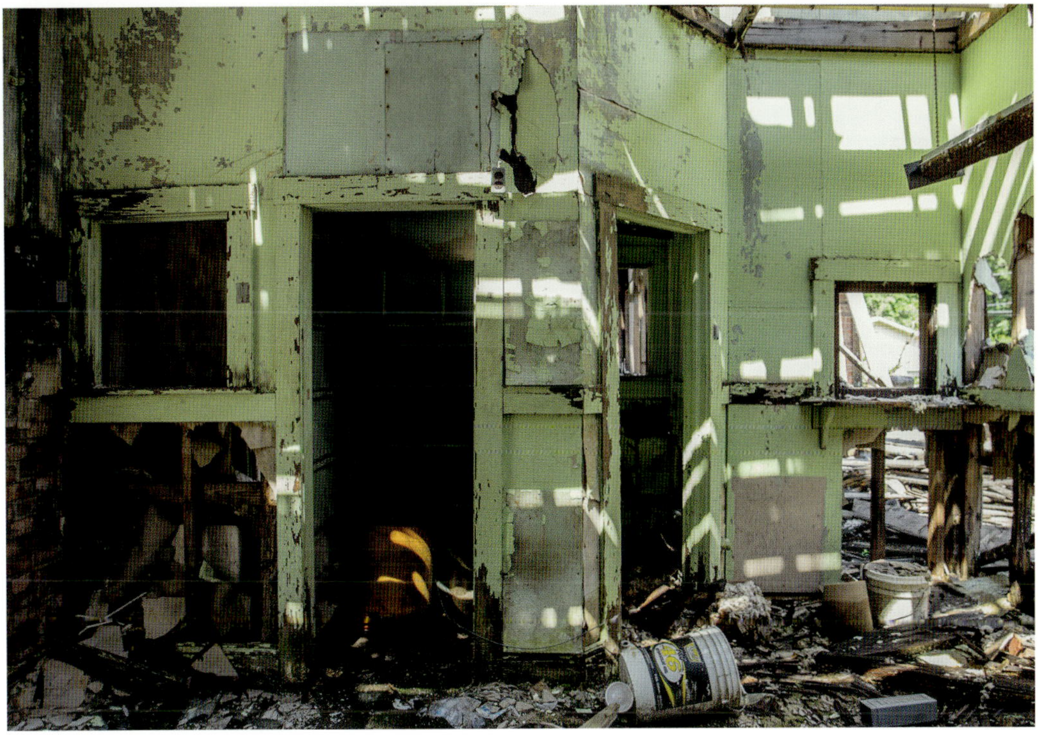

The interior of the station.

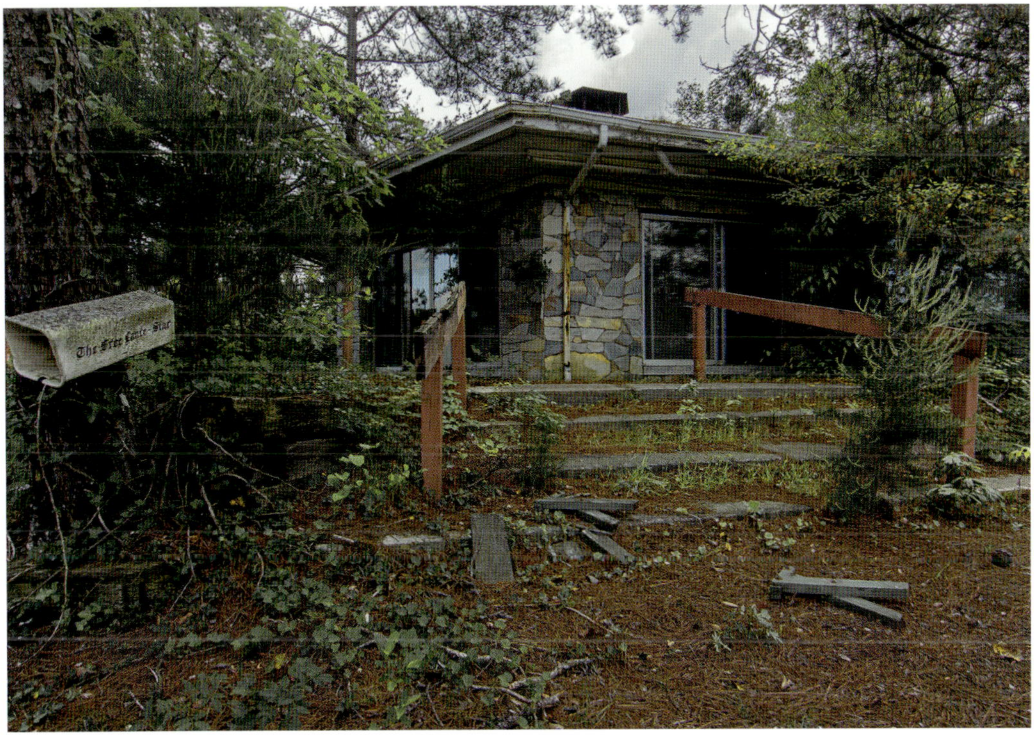

Entrance to the office building of an old roadside motel.

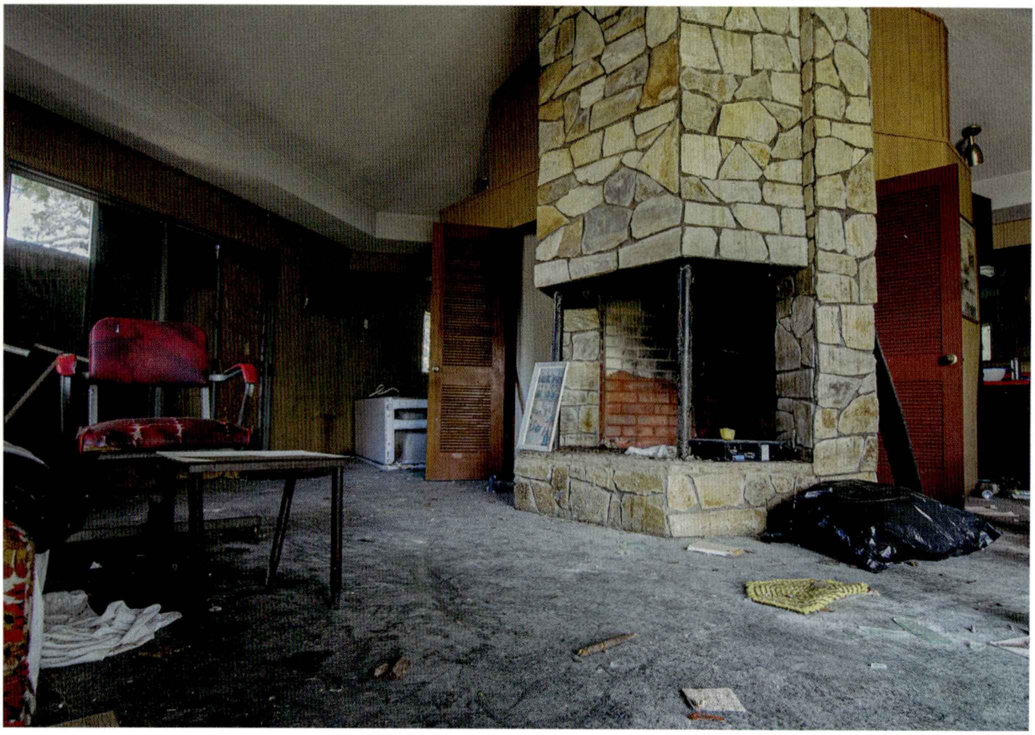

The main lobby with a fireplace, where guests checked in.

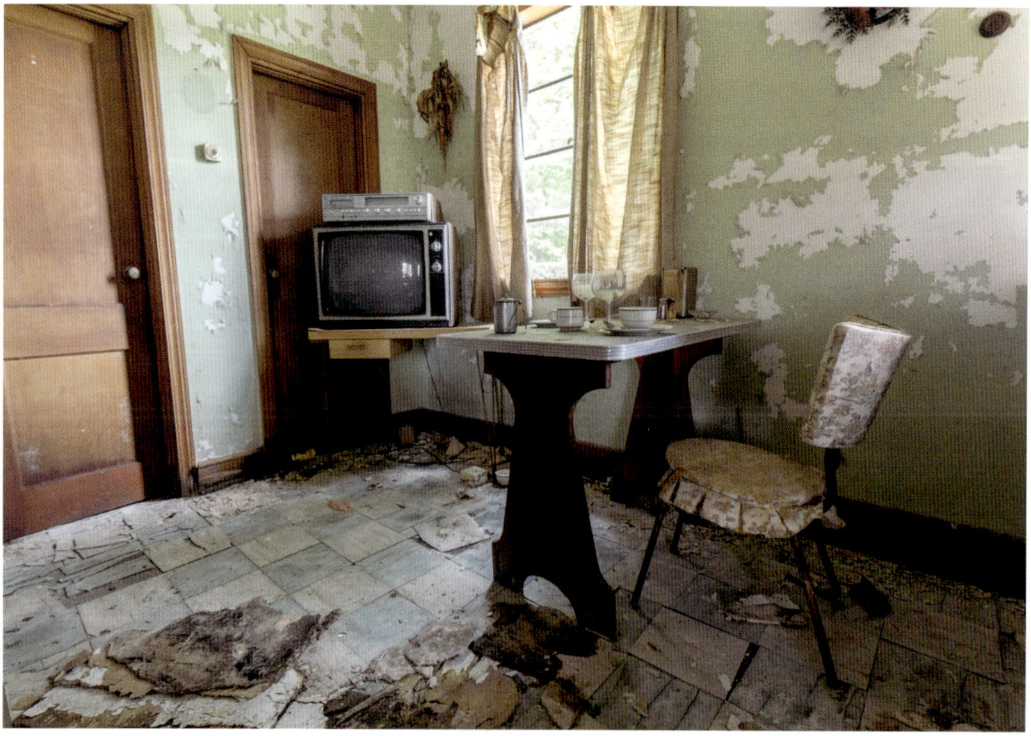

This room featured a table set and ready for dinner by the tv.

9

ABANDONED COUNTRY MOTEL

While we were out scouting some other abandoned locations, we spotted this motel tucked away in the woods, barely visible from the road. It took us a few tries to find a way over to it. Several of the structures were burned and unidentifiable. Our guesses are that they may have been the restaurant or office for the motel. There were several cottages along with an L-shaped motel building. Unfortunately, there isn't any information on this location. It's a great example of how a building just fades into history as nature reclaims it.

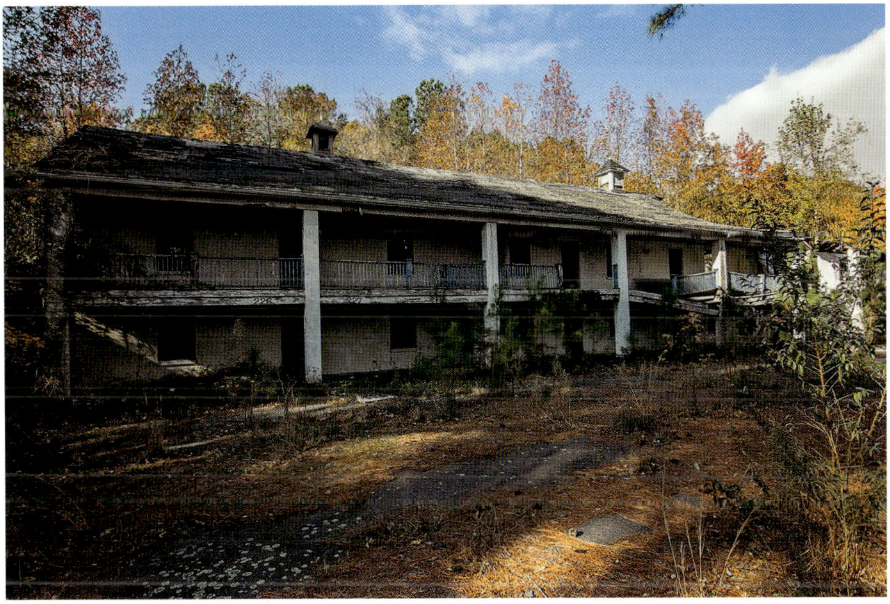

The main hotel building.

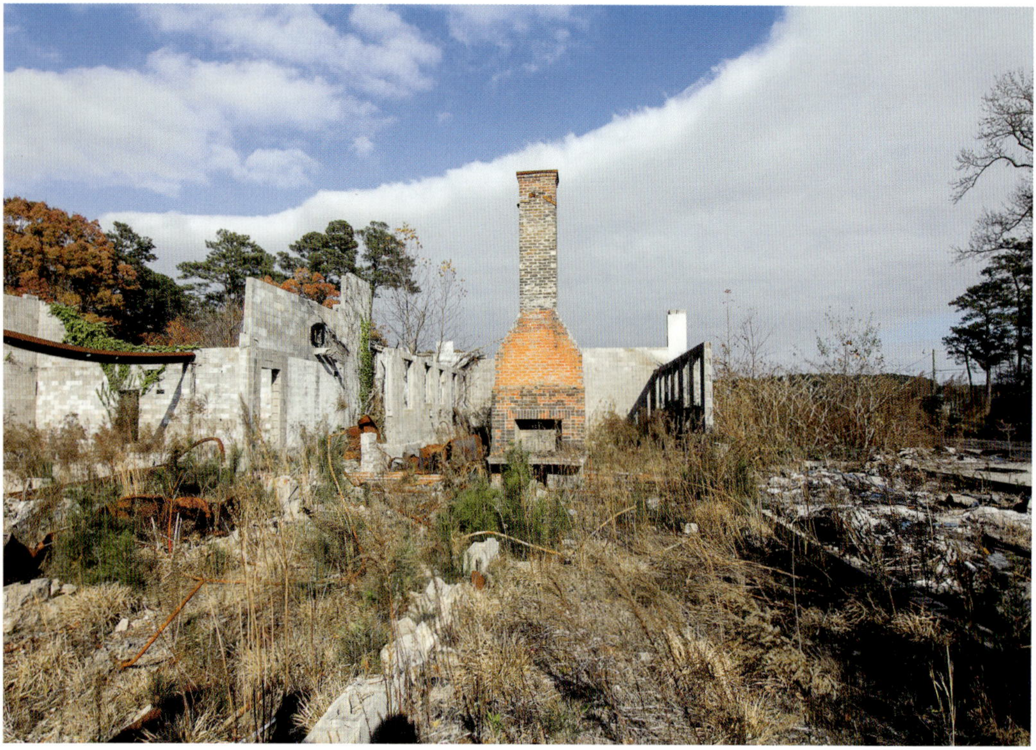

The chimney remains of the burned-down building.

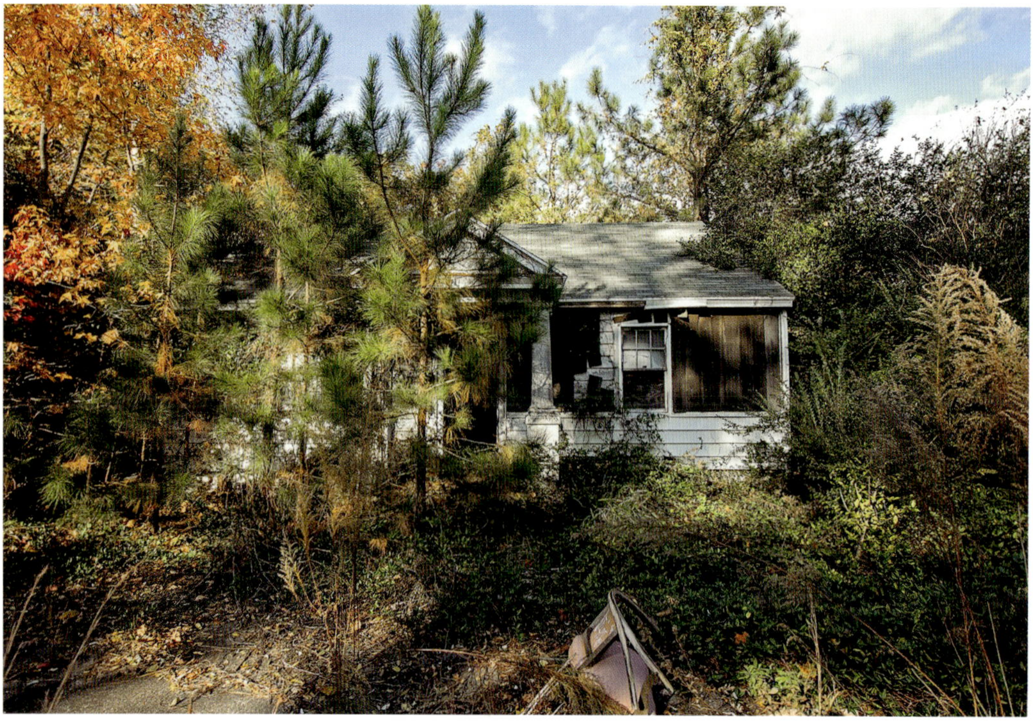

One of the remaining private cottages.

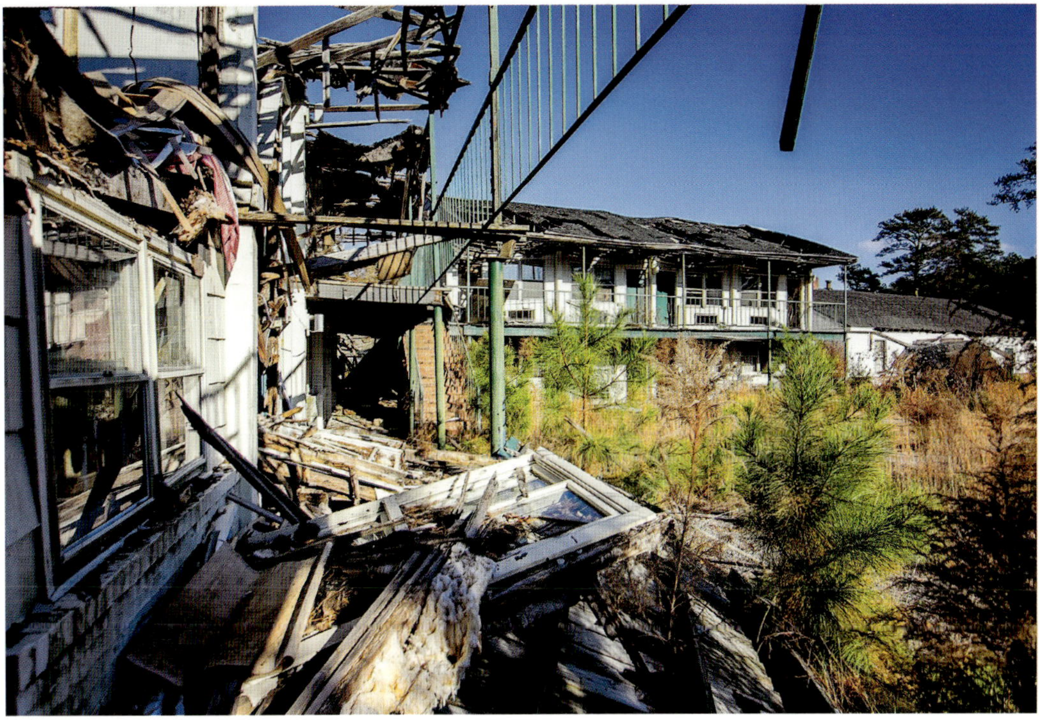

The exterior slowly collapses over the years.

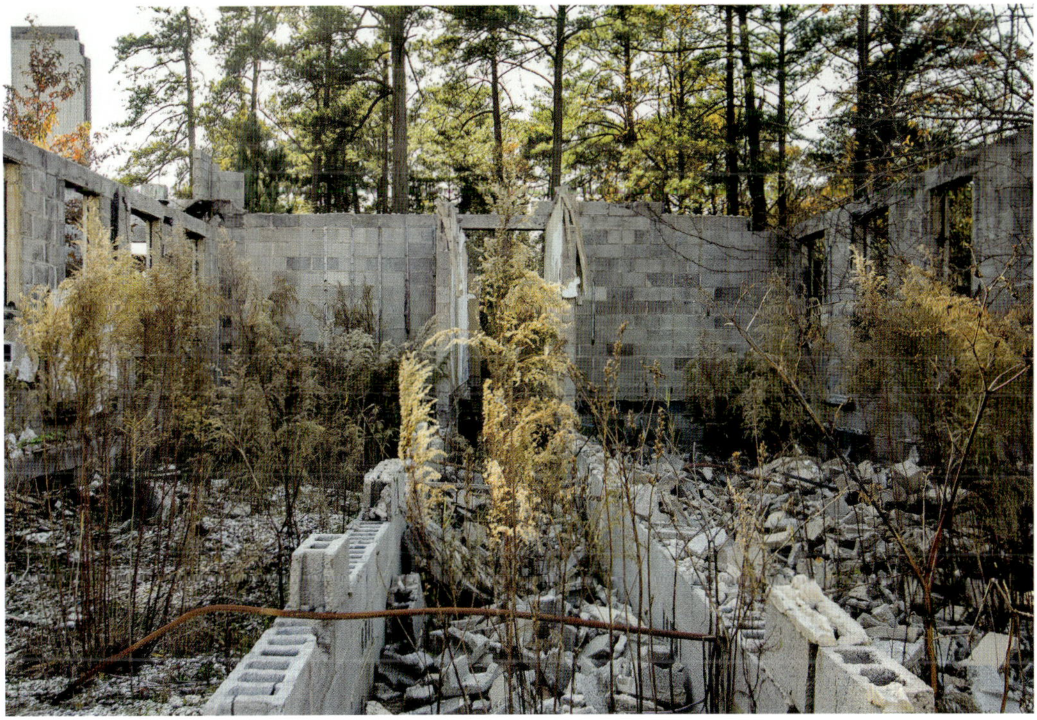

What remains of the burned-down building. It may have been the restaurant.

SOURCES

citymetric.com/transport/route-66-built-communities-interstate-system-destroyed-them-again-4040

crdl.usg.edu/export/html/vrc/pec/crdl_vrc_pec_100.html?Welcome

Feuer, A.B. (1999). *The U.S. Navy in World War I: combat at sea and in the air.* Westport, CT: Greenwood Publishing Group.

ggwash.org/view/69192/liberty-at-lorton-how-a-notorious-old-virginia-prison-got-a-new-life-as-housing

richmondbizsense.com/2019/06/14/remediation-begin-fulton-gas-works-site-city-looks-highest-best-use/

richmondgov.com/PublicUtilities/FultonGasWorks.aspx

smeco.coop/about/history

upress.virginia.edu/title/1357

virginiahistory.org/collections-and-resources/virginia-history-explorer/industrialization-virginia

virginiahistory.org/learn/story-of-virginia/chapter/growth-industry

wikipedia.org/wiki/Lorton_Reformatory

ABOUT THE AUTHOR

DAVE BENTLEY was born and raised in Southwest Virginia, in the foothills of the Appalachian Mountains. Growing up in the country spurred his love and interest of being outdoors and exploring, whether it was hiking through the mountains or exploring old houses and barns. The beautiful mountains and the picturesque countryside helped spark his love of photography. Since then, Dave has continued to advance his photography skills through darkroom and film development courses in college, various workshops, and hours spent watching tutorials online. Currently, Dave resides in Arizona, where he loves exploring the old ghost towns, and photographing the beautiful landscape of the American Southwest.

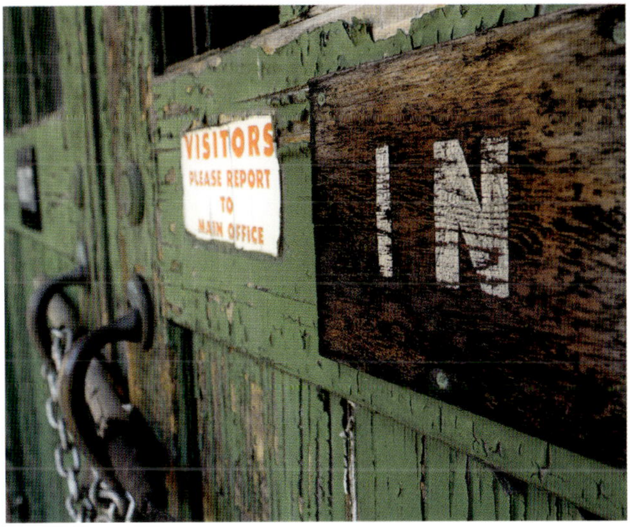

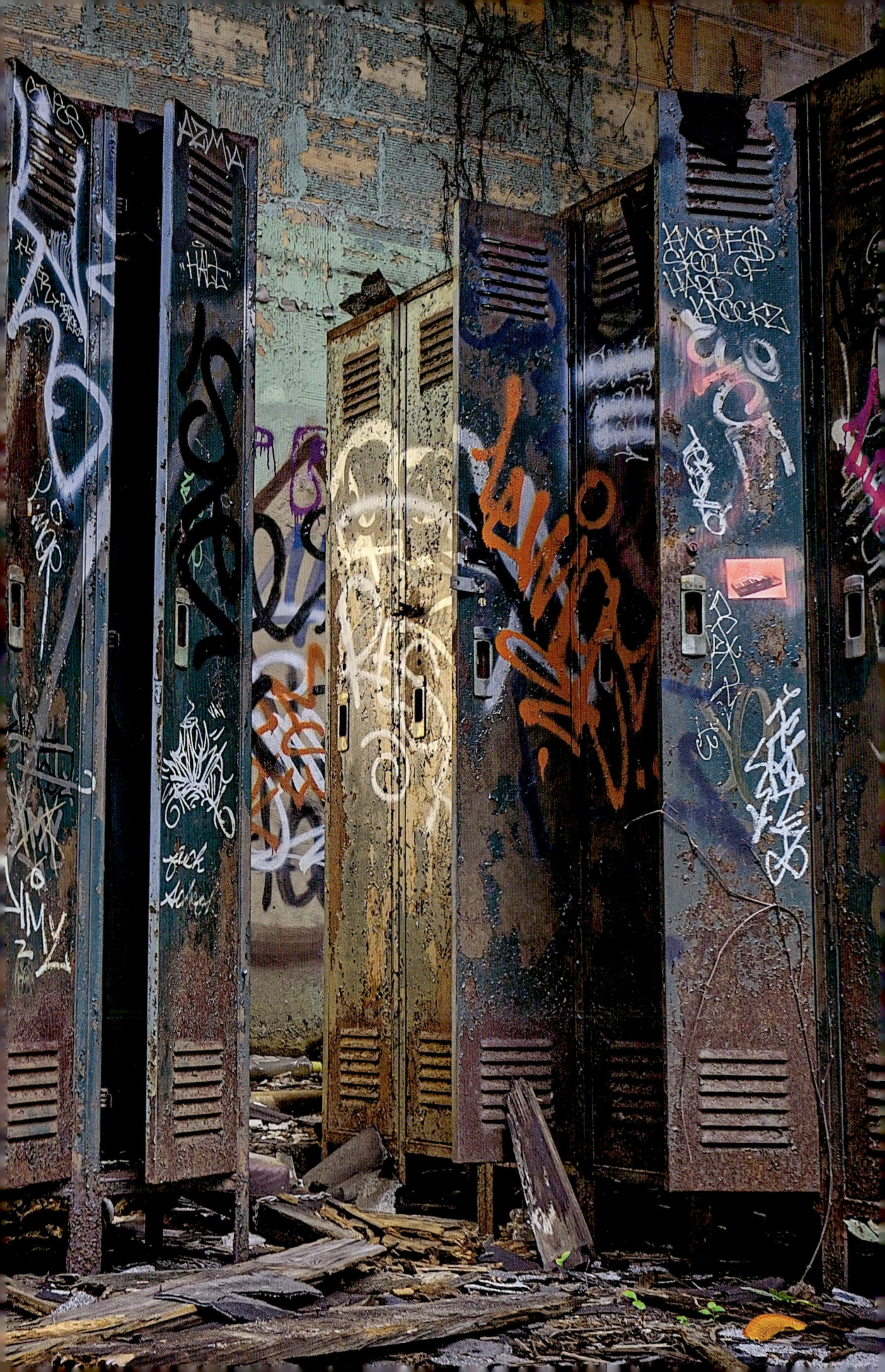